Top 25 locator map
(continues on inside
back cover)
◄

KT-382-446

TwinPack
Tenerife

ANDREW SANGER

Andrew Sanger is a well-
established travel journalist
who has contributed to a wide
range of popular magazines
and most British newspapers.
He is the author of many travel
guides, including *AA Explorer
Israel*, *AA Esssential Lanzarote
and Fuerteventura*, and
*AA TwinPack Lanzarote and
Fuerteventura*.

If you have any comments
or suggestions for this guide
you can contact the editor at
Twinpacks@theAA.com

AA Publishing
Find out more about AA Publishing and
the wide range of services the AA provides
by visiting our website at *www.theAA.com*

Contents

About this book

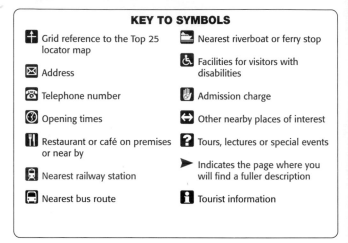

KEY TO SYMBOLS

➕ Grid reference to the Top 25 locator map

✉ Address

☎ Telephone number

🕐 Opening times

🍴 Restaurant or café on premises or near by

🚉 Nearest railway station

🚌 Nearest bus route

⛴ Nearest riverboat or ferry stop

♿ Facilities for visitors with disabilities

✋ Admission charge

↔ Other nearby places of interest

❓ Tours, lectures or special events

➤ Indicates the page where you will find a fuller description

ℹ Tourist information

TwinPack Tenerife is divided into six sections to cover the six most important aspects of your visit to Tenerife. It includes:

- The author's view of the island and its people
- Suggested walks and excursions
- The Top 25 Sights to visit
- Features about different aspects of the island that make it special
- Detailed listings of restaurants, hotels, shops and nightlife
- Practical information

In addition, easy-to-read side panels provide fascinating extra facts and snippets, highlights of places to visit and invaluable practical advice.

CROSS-REFERENCES
To help you make the most of your visit, cross-references, indicated by ➤, show you where to find additional information about a place or subject.

MAPS
The fold-out map in the wallet at the back of the book is a large-scale island map of Tenerife.
The Top 25 locator maps found on the inside front and back covers of the book itself are for quick reference. They show the Top 25 Sights, described on pages 24–48, which are clearly plotted by number (**1** – **25**, not page number) in alphabetical order.

PRICES
Where appropriate, an indication of the cost of an establishment is given by £ signs: £££ denotes higher prices, ££ denotes average prices, while £ denotes lower charges.

TENERIFE
Island life

A Personal View

It's all too easy to think of Tenerife simply as sun and sea and holiday fun. After all, it's Europe's most popular winter sun destination, and attracts many visitors in summer, too. A busy tourism promotion department works hard to encourage more and more people to come here. Year round, tourists outnumber island residents by more than six to one. So it is forgivable to think of Tenerife as nothing more or less than an affordable, satisfying break.

The layer of tourism that clings to the island's rugged surface is no bad thing. Apart from giving the islanders an income, it is following a 100-year-old tradition, and provides millions of people with a lot of pleasure. Most visitors stay in the rainless, sun-baked southern parts of the island where locals have never lived, and usually remain there throughout their stay. The wetter,

more fertile north, where Tenerife's towns and villages have developed over the centuries, attracts fewer visitors. So tourism, while never harmless, does surprisingly little damage to the island's social and physical fabric.

The beach curves into Playa de las Américas.

But beneath all that commercialism there is something more enduring. Peel back the layer of tourism and you will discover that Tenerife is not just a holiday isle. It has a vibrant life and a vivid colonial history of its own, barely more than glimpsed by the sun-seeking crowds. Here is a Spain we don't see much on the mainland: a reminder of the *conquistadores*, an immediate sense of Spain's enterprise, power and wealth centuries ago. Like some of the other Canaries, the island of Tenerife feels very close in spirit and in character to the colonies in Latin America, where so many Tinerfeíos – natives of Tenerife – went to live.

Here, as well, is the Spain of today. Take a side turn, explore the villages, get into the hills, or the backstreets of Santa Cruz or La Laguna,

and holiday land seems to vanish like morning mist. Gone are the menus depicting photographs of the world's favourite dishes, or the waiters who can chat up a *turista* in five languages. Here instead are the real bars and *restaurantes*, the plazas and glazed tiles and the sounds and the people of the Iberian peninsula.

Traditional dress during the romeria or local pilgrimage, held in May

However, that too can be peeled back. There is yet another, more awesome level to Tenerife. Somehow the Teide volcano rising aloof from the centre of the island is its most fitting symbol. Leave the villages and backstreets behind, walk alone in the balmy, luxuriant hills, or in the desolate Casadas. Leave behind the voices and traffic. Take a path among the flowers and the grasses blowing in the Atlantic wind, or in the shadow of the looming cone of Pico del Teide. The Guanches are long gone, but there's an air of mystery about Tenerife that these native islanders bequeathed. Through them, I see that Tenerife belongs neither to the tourist nor to the Spanish, but to the ocean, to Africa, and to the simmering snow-capped volcano which gave the island its Guanche name.

7

Tenerife in Figures

Geography
- Tenerife lies in the western half of the Canary Islands archipelago, just 500km north of the Tropic of Cancer.
- Though Spanish, Tenerife is much closer to the Sahara than Spain – only around 300km from the coast of Africa, but 1,500km from Spain.
- In the centre of the island is the Pico de Teide (3,718m), the highest point of the Atlantic Islands.
- The last volcanic activity took place in 1909 when Mount Chinyero erupted.
- La Gomera lies 32km from Tenerife's southwestern shore.
- The largest of the Canary Islands, Tenerife covers 2,057sq km. It's 130km across at its widest point, and 90km from north to south.
- La Gomera is the second-smallest of the Canaries, measuring just 23km by 25km.

Administration
- Santa Cruz is the chief town of the westerly province Santa Cruz de Tenerife.

People
- Only 700,000 people live on Tenerife, and about 20,000 on La Gomera. They are outnumbered annually by 4 million tourists.
- The population density on Tenerife is more than three times that of mainland Spain.
- The largest town on Tenerife is Santa Cruz with a population of 205,000, followed by La Laguna (127,000) and La Orotava (36,000).
- Spanish is the official language of the islands, with a few indigenous words still in use.

Climate
- In Northern coastal regions the average annual rainfall is around 500mm; in the central regions it rises to 600–800mm; and in the mountains falls to 300mm.
- Average daily temperatures are about 25°C in summer and 19°C in winter.
- Water temperatures are around 19°C in winter and may reach 22°C in summer.
- In July and August the weather pattern can be affected by heatwaves from the Sahara.

People of Tenerife

Christopher Columbus

By far the most famous person associated with La Gomera is Christopher Columbus (1451–1506), the explorer and entrepreneur who stayed there before setting out to discover whether a westward trade route existed to the Indies. His first visit in 1492 was for the purpose of making final checks and supplies before the pioneering Atlantic crossing. Becoming friendly with the island's countess Beatriz de Bobadilla, he visited La Gomera twice during his Atlantic voyages.

Beatriz de Bobadilla

A great beauty at the Spanish court, Beatriz (*c*1455–1508) was a mistress of Ferdinand V, whose queen, Isabella of Castile, contrived to remove her to La Gomera. She married its governor, Count Hernán Peraza, who was murdered by the Guanches for his cruelty. Beatriz took revenge on the native Gomerans and had hundreds put to death or sold into slavery. She continued to rule La Gomera in her own right. In 1498 she married Alonso Fernández de Lugo, conqueror of Tenerife. She was eventually summoned back to court in Madrid, where she was poisoned (almost certainly on the orders of Queen Isabella).

Tomás de Iriarte

The small population of Tenerife, largely illiterate until the 1970s, has produced few famous sons. One of the most important was 18th-century satirical writer and translator Tomás de Iriarte (1750–91), whose works were highly successful on the mainland. They included a collection of fables, *Fábulas Literarias*, and translations of Horace.

Horatio Nelson

Horatio Nelson's (1758–1805) attack on Santa Cruz in 1797 was the only failure of his illustrious career in the service of the British Crown. Then rear admiral, he was sent to seize treasure offloaded by a Spanish ship, but his forces were insufficient for the task; Nelson lost his right arm in the process.

THE FRANCO CONNECTION

General Francisco Franco, the dictator who ruled Spain with an iron hand from 1939 to 1975, launched his coup from Tenerife, where he lived as Capitán-Generale for four months in 1936. For old times' sake he took a holiday on the island in 1953 .

A memorial to General Franco, on the waterfront of Santa Cruz

A Chronology

2–20 million years ago	Volcanic eruptions create the Canary Islands; Tenerife appears 10 million years ago.
c500 BC	Tenerife is peopled by the Guanches (Old Canarian meaning 'son of Tenerife'), believed to have been Berbers, nomadic pastoralists of North Africa.
12th–1st century BC	Phoenician and other sailors visit the Canary Islands. From antiquity the archipelago is known as the Fortunate Isles. On behalf of the Romans, Juba II of Mauritania sends an expedition *c*25 BC to explore the Fortunate Isles. One island is named Canaria for its wild dogs (Latin *canis*, dog); the islands take the name Canaries.
1312	Genoese sailor Lancelotto Malocello visits Fuerteventura and Lanzarote (which is a corruption of his name), the first European colonist in the Canaries.
1402	Two Norman adventurers, Gadifer de la Salle and Jean de Béthencourt, set out to conquer the Canaries. Although only taking Lanzarote, they claim all the islands for the king of Spain, who financed their trip.
Early 1400s	On more easterly islands, Norman and Spanish settlers enslave the Guanche natives and build European-style farming villages, but Tenerife remains unconquered.
1493–95	Spanish colonist, Alonso Fernández de Lugo, financed by Genoese merchants, attacks Tenerife. Most of his men are ambushed and killed by the Guanches a year later. In November 1494 de Lugo returns with more men and conquers the island, killing thousands of Guanches. Land handed out to investors in his expedition is developed as sugar plantations. Portuguese and Spanish labourers are shipped in to work the new farms.
16–17th centuries	Destructive French, English, Dutch and Arab pirates and privateers harass Tenerife, attracted

by the laden merchant ships coming from the New World, pausing at Santa Cruz. Tenerife's various fortifications date from this period.

18th century	Grapes are planted and soon wine is an important product. Tenerife becomes a civilised and cultured hideaway for European nobility and wealthy traders.
1797	Horatio Nelson attacks Santa Cruz in order to take the town (► 9).
19th century	The wine trade collapses, but is replaced first by the cultivation of cochineal beetles (for their dye), which are raised on plantations of cacti, and then by bananas, soon the main crop. The banana boats also carry passengers, and the island becomes a fashionable resort for wealthy British scholars, writers and artists. One of the first guidebooks is written – *Tenerife and its Six Satellites* (by Olivia Stone, 1887).
1914–18	The Great War causes massive emigration.
1936	Francisco Franco, military governor or Capitán-General of the Canary Islands, based on Tenerife, plans a right-wing coup to take over Spain. On 18 July, the Spanish Civil War (1936–39) starts with the Nationalist takeover of Tenerife. A week later Franco has control of all the Canaries. He leaves Tenerife for Morocco, and launches an attack on the Spanish mainland.
Early 1960s	Package tourism to the Canaries begins. Puerto de la Cruz is transformed into a modern resort.
1978	International airport Reina Sofía opens on the south coast. Playa de las Américas begins to be developed.
1980–90s	Tourism reaches huge proportions and becomes the island's main source of income.
2000	Plans are made to take tourism upmarket and reduce visitor numbers.

11

Best of Tenerife

Enjoy a Canarian wine

If you only have a short time to visit Tenerife, or would like to get a really complete picture of the island, here are the essentials:

- Go up Pico del Teide, the high point of Tenerife, a snow-capped dormant volcano. From here you can see almost the whole of the Canary Islands (➤ 42).
- Experience Playa de las Américas. Leave the real world behind and enter the package holiday dreamland, in a purpose-built town of artificial beaches, all-night discos, English pubs and restaurants that proudly boast 'No Spanish Food Served Here!' (➤ 43).
- Go bananas. Eat Tenerife bananas, have them flambéed for dessert, drink banana liqueur, buy souvenirs made of banana leaves and visit Bananera El Guanche (➤ 24).
- Eat a Canarian stew. Try *potaje*, *rancho canario* or *puchero* – vegetables and meat simmered to a savoury perfection. With bread, locals consider it a complete meal.
- Get spicy. You must try the pleasantly spicy local sauce called *mojo*. Served with fish or *papas arrugadas* (wrinkly potatoes), it's the most Canarian thing on the menu.
- Drink a local wine. One of the first big successes for colonial Tenerife was the development of drinkable wines to rival those in mainland Spain.
- Get out of the resorts. Walk, drive or cycle, but one way or another see the Tenerife most tourists miss.
- Watch a whale. Join one of the boat excursions to see the whales and dolphins which live just off southern Tenerife and La Gomera (➤ 79).
- Have fun at a fiesta. It's an unusual fortnight in the Tenerife calendar that doesn't have at least one fiesta.
- Go to another island. Take the ferry to La Gomera for the truly unspoiled Canaries. If you're staying on La Gomera, take the boat trip over just to visit Pico del Teide.

The May romeria *festival in Santa Cruz*

TENERIFE
how to organise your time

A Walk Around Santa Cruz

Start in the waterfront Plaza de España, dominated by its Civil War memorial and the massive Palacio Insular (► 47), in which the tourist office and council authorities are housed.

Walk into the adjoining square, Plaza de la Candelaria. This agreeable pedestrianised square (► 58) has good bars, craft shops and sights, including the Banco Español de Credito in the charming 18th-century Palacio de Carta.

At the end of the square, continue on Calle del Castillo. This is the main shopping street of Santa Cruz, a colourful avenue of little shops with gaudy signs, 'bazaars' and crowds of tourists and locals.

Continue to Plaza de Weyler. There's an Italian white marble fountain at the centre of this popular square. To one side stands the Capitanía General, where Franco lived while he was based here.

Locals and tourists enjoy the shops, cafés and restaurants in Calle del Castillo, Santa Cruz

At the northern tip of the square, turn along Calle Méndez Núñez. This less interesting street soon leads to the Parque Municipal García Sanabria, an enjoyable place to get away from street noise and relax on the tiled public benches among greenery.

Take Calle del Pilar, opposite the park's south side. Follow this street to Plaza del Príncipe. In the slightly raised square, once the friary garden of a Franciscan monastery, luxuriant laurel trees shade a bandstand. To one side the Municipal Fine Arts Museum (► 52) occupies the former monastery, alongside its church, the Iglesia de San Francisco (► 53). Calle de Béthencourt leads the short distance back to Plaza de España.

A Drive in the Northern Hills

Allow a full day to explore the mountainous northern reaches of the island. This is the part which is paradoxically both the most and the least developed, with big working towns on the coast and in the valleys, the simplest hamlets scattered across the upper slopes, and breathtaking panoramic views from the hill crests.

Begin the drive at Santa Cruz, or join at Tacoronte or at any point on the route if coming from the west or south.

Head north for 8km on the coastal highway to San Andrés and the Playa de las Teresitas. Turn inland for 10km on TF112, the twisting, climbing road to El Bailadero.

You're now climbing into the Anaga Mountains (▶ 15, 54). El Bailadero is a magnificent viewpoint, with sweeping vistas of mountain and coast.

Take the high cumbre (ridge or crest) road, TF1123, towards Mount Taborno. At the fork after 7km, take the summit road.

A succession of views along this high road includes Mount Taborno's spectacular Mirador Pico del Inglés (a few metres up a side turn on the left). Continue along the crest road, with more viewpoints, notably at Cruz del Carmen, where there is a 17th-century chapel and a restaurant.

After Las Mercedes take the right turn at Las Canteras on TF121 to Tejina. At Tejina, follow TF122 as it turns left towards Tacoronte. 7km beyond Tejina, 1km after Valle de Guerra, pause at the Casa de Carta.

The island's remarkable Anthropology Museum is set in the Casa de Carta (▶ 34), a restored 17th-century farmhouse. Continue on this road to Tacoronte, the wine town. Leave town on the eastbound *autopista* to return to Santa Cruz.

INFORMATION

Distance 90km
Time 4 hours
Start/end point Santa Cruz
🚻 Mirador Cruz del Carmen
(££)

The view from the Mirador de Jardina to Pico del Ingles, in the Anaga Mountains

A Walk Around Puerto

INFORMATION

Distance 2km
Time 1½ hours
Start point Plaza de Iglesia
End point Lago Martiánez
🍽 Plaza del Charco (£–££)

The church tower keeps time in Plaza Iglesia.

Shoreline colour near the Casa de la Real Aduana

Despite the tourist crowds, Puerto retains an atmosphere of grace and history. Much of the central area is pedestrianised, making it enjoyable to walk in the streets of this old colonial town.

Start from Plaza de la Iglesia, a handsome and popular old main square with palms and greenery, a lovely swan fountain, dominated by the church (➤ 53).

Take Calle de Cologán (away from the sea) and turn into the second right, Calle Iriarte. Reaching Plaza Concejil and Calle San Juan, you'll find the elegant balconied 18th-century house Casa Iriarte to the right, now a souvenir and craft shop and an amateur naval museum. On your left is the landmark Palacio Ventosa, with its tall tower.

Continuing along Calle Iriarte , turn right into Calle Blanco. This brings you to Plaza del Charco, the pleasantly bustling and shaded heart of town (➤ 59).

Take Calle de San Felipe from the northwest corner of the square. This street has unpretentious restaurants and old Canarian buildings of character. Turn right and right again into Calle de Lomo, for the Museo Arqueológico (➤ 52).

Retrace your steps to Plaza del Charco, then turn left on Calle Blanco towards the sea. Here is the Puerto Pesquero (➤ 59), the endearing little harbour with the modest black-and-white Casa de la Real Aduana (Royal Customs House) on one corner.

Follow the main seashore road (Calle de Santo Domingo) eastward past Punta del Viento (Windy Point), eventually reaching Calle San Telmo. Pause to admire the tiny Ermita de San Telmo (➤ 58). Continue to the Lago Martiánez (➤ 30).

A Drive Around Western Tenerife

This day out takes in all the grandeur of Tenerife's volcanic heartland.

Leave Puerto de la Cruz on the motorway heading towards Santa Cruz, but exit at junction 11 (Tacoronte) for La Esperanza.

La Esperanza is popular for lunch and a walk in the high pine woods of the Bosque de la Esperanza, just south on C824. This road is the Carretera Dorsal running along the mountainous 'spine' of the island. Take C824 south from La Esperanza. The road rises through pine woods, often shrouded in clouds or mist.

At a bend, a sign points the way to the Las Raíces monument, marking the spot where Franco met army officers to plan their coup. Pause at the Mirador Pico de las Flores and other viewpoints for dramatic views of the north coast. Eventually the road passes the observatory at Izaña and enters the national park.

INFORMATION

Distance 145km
Time 4 hours
Start/end point Puerto de la Cruz
🍴 Restaurants near El Portillo and the *parador*

Banana plantations in the La Orotava Valley

Follow C824 to the junction with the C821 and follow this to the left, continuing south. The Centro de Visitantes , at El Portillo pass, marks the entrance to the Caldera de las Cañadas . After 11km of volcanic terrain you reach the Pico del Teide cable car (► 42) and 4km further, the *parador*, nearly opposite Los Roques de García.

At Boca del Tauce, the typical Cañadas scenery abruptly ends. Return through the park to the Centro de Visitantes at El Portillo.

Beyond El Portillo, take the left-hand fork down into the Valle de la Orotava, passing through heath, vines and, on the lowest level, bananas. Continue the descent into Puerto de la Cruz.

A Walk up Pico del Teide

INFORMATION

Distance 8km
Time 6–7 hours
Start point From C821
    Montaña Blanca bus stop
End point Top cable-car
    station (La Rambleta)

🍴 Take a picnic (no food or
    water on route). Bar at La
    Rambleta

ℹ️ Centro de Visitantes,
    El Portillo

The ascent of Pico del Teide is the most exhilarating walk on Tenerife – though it's only suitable for fit, experienced ramblers. Take plenty of water and warm clothes, and start as early as possible, checking the weather forecast and that the cable car is running for the return journey (➤ 42).

Start from the main road C821 at the start of the track to Montaña Blanca. At first the track passes through a desolate volcanic terrain of sharp, gritty pebbles. After an hour or an hour

and a half, you reach the old Montaña Blanca car park.

Follow the sign indicating the Refugio de Altavista, which starts you on a steeper climb on a sandy track. Climb for about 2 hours along this path to reach the *refugio*, or mountain refuge – which may or may not be open (usually open daily 5PM to 10AM). Continue on the path, the edge of which is clearly marked.

Some 3 hours later, the path becomes stonier, but more level. Eventually you reach the path that leads from the top cable-car station to the summit. To complete the ascent you need a permit (➤ 42).

In a wild landscape of multicoloured volcanic rock and scree, the path becomes a steep scramble.

You'll pass sulphurous steam holes emitting heat and vapour from the ground. The views are phenomenal. The summit is marked by a crucifix, where sometimes elderly local women come to say a prayer, seemingly climbing here with ease. Return to the cable-car station and take the car down to the road.

Pico del Teide and the landscape of the national park

A Drive in the South

Leave the resorts behind, climbing into near-barren sun-baked landscapes. From Los Cristianos take the Arona road, C622 (changes to C822 after the *autopista* junction). Pass through the village of Valle de San Lorenzo to reach Mirador de la Centinela for a sweeping view over a landscape of volcanic cones.

About 2km further on, minor road 5114 turns left towards Vilaflor. It climbs steeply in places, eventually reaching the 5112 at Escalona, where you turn right to continue climbing. The road skirts Montaña del Pozo (1,294m). Along here walled vineyard terraces climb the slopes to Vilaflor (► 54), the highest village in the Canaries, noted for its white wines.

On reaching Vilaflor, turn left onto the C821 and keep climbing. Above the village, past the Ermita de San Roque, pause at the Mirador de San Roque for a tremendous view. Almost at once the road enters the fragrant pine forest that encircles the Cañadas region. A twisting mountain road through the forest gives more *mirador* views as Pico del Teide comes into view.

The road leaves the forest and at Boca del Tauce enters the volcanic Caldera de las Cañadas (► 42). Take a left onto the C823 for Chío. The road cuts across a dark landscape of cones and lava flows. Eventually you reach the pine forests once more. There's a pleasant picnic site and rest area (*zona recreativa*) near Chío. The road descends sharply. Before Chío there are good views down to the sea, with La Gomera visible across the water.

At Chío junction turn left and left again onto the C822. Pass unspoiled little Guía de Isora. Cross a succession of *barrancos* (gorges), eventually reaching the Autopista del Sur. Take Exit 27 or 28 for Los Cristianos.

INFORMATION

Distance 106km
Time 3 hours driving
Start point Los Cristianos
🍴 El Mirador (££)
 ✉ Mirador de San Roque, Vilaflor
🍴 Las Estrellas (££)
 ✉ Just before Chío

Top: cultivated terraces in Vilaflor, the highest village on Tenerife
Bottom: the Caldera de las Cañadas beyond Los Roques de Garcia

Finding Peace & Quiet

Despite Tenerife's clamour and crowds, much of the island remains tranquil – it is easy to escape from the excesses of tourism. Remember too that most tourists wake up late: even popular spots enjoy relative peace in the mornings.

The desert-like south possesses a magical quality of stillness and silence. In the central uplands, pine-covered slopes reach into a rocky terrain carved by the volcanic power of Pico del Teide. The lush green northern hills, draped with perennial wild blossom, are a delight that few visitors discover. Almost anywhere off the beaten track, the country is coloured with masses of nasturtiums and hibiscus, marigolds and carnations, geraniums and hanging bougainvillea.

Quiet country paths are a feature of the island, and make a pleasant break for an interesting stroll, getting to know Tenerife's character and landscapes. Keen ramblers could spend a fortnight on the island and barely see another foreigner, taking more isolated trails to climb and explore the interior. You don't need to be a strong walker to discover all this. Car drivers will soon find picnic spots away from the main roads. ICONA, Spain's environmental protection organisation, has created beautifully located picnic places all over the island. Some 1,700 species of plantlife flourish here, with much of the fauna and flora being unique to the island. It's worth adding that Tenerife is mercifully free of troublesome insects, and there are no poisonous snakes.

On the dry southern shores, cacti and palms thrive, while along the northern and western coasts, semi-tropical varieties abound. Here are woods of mimosa, jacaranda and rubber trees, wild roses and poinsettia, and, of course, that Tenerife marvel, the mighty Dragon Tree (Dracaena draco) and the gentle bird-of-paradise flower (Strelitzia).

Top: wildflowers on Tenerife
Bottom: cacti in the Parques Exóticos near Los Cristoanos

The centre of Tenerife, in and around the Teide National Park, contrasts the greenery of the Orotava Valley with the drama of Las Cañadas and the intriguing rare plants of Pico del Teide. The most striking is the giant bugloss (*Echium wildpretii*) with amazing erect red flower clusters as much as two metres long – a true native found only on the Canary Islands. High on the slopes, the Teide violet (*Viola cheiranthifolia*) lives only here. The Teide daisy and Teide broom, too, are endemic. The mountainsides are covered with pine and palm. On upper slopes pockets survive of the once extensive *Laurisilva*, or forests of Canary laurel (*Larus canariensis*).

Take a boat to La Gomera. From San Sebastián, where the ferry disembarks, head west into the interior of this undeveloped Canary Island, deeply scored with *barrancos* (gorges). Its central mountain region is thickly covered with Canary laurel forest, and on the coasts it is still possible to find sun, sea – and solitude.

On the road to Agulo, La Gomera, with Pico del Teide on the horizon

The landscape of Teide National Park

21

What's On

JANUARY	*Cabalgata de los Reyes Magos* (The Three Kings Cavalcade, 5–6 Jan): many places, especially Santa Cruz and Valle Gran Rey (La Gomera)
	Local fiestas (17–22 Jan): Garachico, Icod de los Vinos, Los Realejos, San Sebastián (La Gomera)
FEBRUARY	*Candelaria* (Candlemas, 2 Feb): festival and pilgrimage in certain towns and villages, especially Candelaria
	Carnæval (one week, early to mid-Feb): Santa Cruz, Puerto de la Cruz – the climax is Shrove Tuesday, the biggest event of the year; (end Feb) Los Cristianos; (end Feb/early Mar) San Sebastián (La Gomera)
MARCH/APRIL	*San José holiday* (19 Mar)
	Semana Santa (Holy Week): all over the islands during Easter Week
	Local fiestas (25 Apr): especially at Icod de los Vinos, Teguesta and Agulo (La Gomera)
MAY/JUNE	*Día de las Islas Canarias* (Canary Islands Day, 30 May): throughout the archipelago
	Corpus Christi (late May/early Jun): Octavo (eight days) of huge celebrations throughout the island, especially La Orotava, La Laguna and Vilaflor
	Romería (post *Corpus Christi*): local pilgrimages
	Fiesta de San Juan (24 Jun): midsummer at Vallehermoso (La Gomera) and other villages
JULY	*Fiestas del Gran Poder* (15 Jul): Puerto de la Cruz – processions, parades, fireworks and fun
	Public holiday (25 Jul): festivities in Santiago
AUGUST	*Asunción and Nuestra Señora de la Candelaria* (Candelaria, 15 Aug): important pilgrimage festival involving whole island
	Romeria de San Roque (Garachico, 16 Aug): popular, colourful local event
	Nuestra Señora del Carmen (Los Cristianos, 30 Aug): lively fiesta
SEPTEMBER	*Semana Colombina* (Columbus Week, 1–6 Sep): San Sebastián (La Gomera)
	Virgen de Buen Paso (15 Sep): Alajeró (La Gomera)
	Local fiestas (mid-Sep): La Laguna, Tacoronte
OCTOBER	*Día de la Hispanidad* (12 Oct): celebrating Columbus
NOVEMBER/DECEMBER	*Holidays:* 1 Nov, 6 Dec, 8 Dec, 25 Dec

TENERIFE's
top 25 sights

The sights are shown on the maps on the inside front cover and inside back cover, numbered **1** – **25** alphabetically

Bananera El Guanche

INFORMATION

✚ C2

✉ 2km from Puerto de la Cruz on the road to La Orotava

☎ 922 331853

🕐 Daily 9–6

♿ Few

💷 Expensive

🍴 Bar on site (£), restaurants in town (£–£££)

🚌 Free bus to Puerto de la Cruz every 20/30 mins daily

Banana liqueur, produced on the local plantation

Bananera El Guanche is a popular family attraction devoted to the subject of the banana – a truly unusual plant

Bananas are a staple of the island economy though the majority are taken by Spain (the Dwarf Cavendish variety cannot be exported due to EU export regulations). Both entertaining and informative, Bananera is set in an old banana farm (*bananera* means banana plantation). A video (every 20 mins) explains the method of banana cultivation, an extraordinarily complicated and arduous process. The banana, you are informed, is not a tree, but a plant, and takes 16–19 months before it produces its first 'hand' of bananas. One of its many peculiarities is that each plant is both male and female, and reproduces without pollination.

Visitors then stroll along a route which takes them through various kinds of banana plants, as well as many other intriguing species. You'll see varieties as diverse as papaya, mango, the huge and ancient *drago* (or dragon tree) species, sugar cane, cotton, coffee, cocoa, peanuts, pineapples and more. Less familiar names include *kapok* and *chirimoya* (custard apples). The cactus garden has hundreds of kinds of cactus, while in the Tropical Plantation there is a wide range of fruit trees as well as *datura*, tobacco and *chicle* – the South American tree from whose milky resin chewing gum is derived. There are exotic flowers too, including elegant, vivid *strelitzia*, or bird of paradise flowers, which have become a symbol of the Canaries. Boxed *strelitzia* flowers are a popular souvenir for Bananera visitors; they can be delivered to your hotel on the day of your flight home.

Finally, before leaving, you're offered a free taste of banana liqueur (powerful – and sweet) and a ripe banana.

Casa de los Balcones

The most famous sight in the sedate, balconied Spanish colonial hilltown of La Orotava is an intriguing 17th-century mansion.

Pretty potted geraniums decorate the balconies looking over Calle San Francisco. It's not the balconies on the outside, though, that give the house its name: enter the impressive front doors and you will find the exquisitely carved wooden balconies of the interior courtyard. Here abundant refreshing greenery, earthenware pots and an old wine press give a cool, elegant air. The building's history is told in the museum upstairs: originally it consisted of two separate houses built in 1632 as homes for prosperous colonists.

Downstairs in the busy souvenir and craft shop, a major stop-off point for coach tours, an additional attraction is local craftspeople demonstrating how to roll a cigar, weave a basket, or paint sand in readiness for the big Corpus Christi celebrations. This unusual shop sells, in addition to popular cheap souvenirs, a wide range of high-quality items such as Spanish and Canarian lace and linen, and traditional hand-crafted Canarian embroideries. Some small items – such as handkerchiefs – give an opportunity to buy good quality local goods at affordable prices.

Some of the embroideries are made on the premises, as the Casa de los Balcones also serves as a highly regarded school for embroidery. For over 50 years the school has been training small numbers of pupils in the traditional methods and designs of Canarian embroidery, which would perhaps have disappeared altogether if not for its efforts.

INFORMATION

- 🔲 D2
- ✉ Calle San Francisco 3, La Orotava
- ☎ 922 330629
- 🕐 Mon–Fri 8:30–6:30, Sat 8:30–5, Sun 8:30–1
- 🚻 None
- 🏛 Museum cheap, craft shop free
- 🍴 Restaurants and bars in Plaza de la Constitución
- 🚌 345 and 350 (Puerto de la Cruz–La Orotava) every 20–30 mins; 348 same route once daily
- 🔲 La Oratava (➤ 25)

A richly embroidered waistcoat from the Casa de los Balcones

25

Drago Milenario

INFORMATION

➕ B2

✉ Parque del Drago (by the church), Plaza de la Constitución 1, Icod de los Vinos

☎ 922 330629

Moderate (free view from church square)

Bars and cafés nearby (£)

354 and 363 (Puerto de la Cruz–Icod) every 30 mins

Icod de los Vinos (➤ 28), Garachico (➤ 27, 52)

Dragon Tree Festival in Sep (Icod)

The *drago* or dragon tree is a species peculiar to the Canary Islands, and this amazing, ancient example has become an island emblem.

Just how old is this extraordinary tree? The age of the 'Thousand-Year-Old Dragon Tree' is often exaggerated to two or even three thousand years. In reality, this majestic specimen, the oldest known, probably dates back about 600 years.

More remarkable perhaps is that the species itself – *Dracaena draco*, closely related to the yucca – has barely evolved since the age of the dinosaurs. It has long been an object of fascination, not just among modern botanists and naturalists, but among all who are sensitive to magic and mystery. That's partly because of its curious form, growing like a bundle of separate trunks clinging together before bursting asunder to create the *drago*'s distinctive mushroom shape. Weirdest of all is the *drago*'s strange resin, which turns as red as blood on contact with the air. Though nothing is known of Guanche beliefs, many people insist that the *drago* was worshipped by these first inhabitants of the island, who did use its resin for embalming.

Standing 17m high and with a diameter of 6m, the Drago Milenario is the main attraction at Icod de los Vinos, an attractive little wine town on the west coast. One of Tenerife's largest Guanche settlements stood here when the Europeans arrived, and the Drago Milenario was already mature when the Spanish took control. The gigantic tree is now protected in gardens while bars and souvenir shops around cash in on the tree's mystique. Different from the rest, and an attraction in itself, is the traditional and pretty shop, Casa del Drago.

The spiky leaves of the Drago Milenario

Garachico

For 200 years, vessels set sail laden with wine and sugar from Garachico, Tenerife's busiest port. Then in one night the harbour was destroyed.

Created as a port by Genoese entrepreneur Cristobal de Ponte in 1496, the original Garachico became a prosperous colonial town and so it remained for two centuries. Now it lies partly buried beneath today's town – on 5 May 1706 the Volcan Negro (just south of the town) roared into life, pouring lava through Garachico and into its harbour.

The islanders laid out new streets on the land formed by the lava. But the harbour – originally much larger – was never to recover, and Garachico, with its fine mansions and cobbled streets, became a handsome relic.

Around the main square, Glorieta de San Francisco, the old Franciscan monastery, Convento de San Francisco, pre-dates the eruption. It now houses the Casa de la Cultura, which hosts events and exhibitions (go inside just to see the pretty interiors and two courtyards), and the Museo de las Ciencias Naturales, a modest mix of local flora, fauna and history. Don't miss the pictures showing the route of the lava flow.

Parque Puerta de Tierra, a lush sunken garden alongside Plaza de Juan González de la Torre, was part of Garachico's harbour. A huge arch which marked the port entrance has been dug out of the lava and re-erected in the square.

For a tremendous view, go up to the roof of Castillo de San Miguel. This dark 16th-century fortress of the counts of Gomera, emblazoned with their crests, stood firm as the lava flowed past. Today it contains a little museum and craft stall. Steps lead down to the sea, where the lava has made pleasing rocky pools.

INFORMATION

- B2
- Calle Esteban de Ponte 5
- ☎ 922 133461
- Isla Baja (££) for fish, and Casa Ramón (£) for Canarian dishes
- 363 (Puerto de la Cruz–Buenavista) hourly
- None
- Icod de los Vinos (➤ 28), Drago Milenario (➤ 26)
- Romería de San Roque, Aug; Feria Artesanía (craft fair) monthly, first Sun
- For the best view of the lava flow that engulfed Garachico take the mountain road (TF1421) up to Mirador de Garachico

Convento de San Francisco

- Glorieta de San Francisco
- Mon–Fri 9–7, Sat 9–6, Sun, hols 9–2
- None
- Moderate

Castillo de San Miguel

- ☎ 922 830000
- Daily 10–6
- None
- Cheap

Icod de los Vinos

INFORMATION

- B2
- Bars and restaurants nearby
- 354, 363 (Puerto de la Cruz–Icod) every 30 mins
- Garachico (➤ 27)
- Big fiestas on 22 Jan, 25 Mar, 24 Jun and 29 Nov; Corpus Christi in Jun; Santa Barbara end Aug; Dragon Tree Festival in Sep

Make your choice at the Casa del Vino

In the hills above Puerto de la Cruz is the pretty town of Icod, whose name means 'the beautiful place of the wines'.

One of the highlights of a tour around Tenerife is the little town of Icod. Its main attraction is the gigantic Dragon Tree known – with poetic licence – as the *Drago Milenario*, the Thousand-Year-Old Dragon Tree (➤ 26).

But the town has other charms too. The Plaza de la Iglesia, apart from its view of the ancient *drago*, has a lovely 15th-century church, the Iglesia de San Marcos, containing a baroque altarpiece, a decorated timber ceiling and a magnificent 2m-tall cross from Mexico, a masterpiece of delicate silverwork. A short distance away, the Mariposario del Drago (Butterfly Garden) is aflutter with colourful tropical butterflies.

As the name makes clear, Icod is also known for its wines. Taste and buy them at shops near Plaza de la Iglesia, such as Casa del Vino or Casa del Drago.

Jardín Botánico

One of the most enjoyable places to pass some time in Puerto de la Cruz is the exuberantly exotic Botanical Garden.

This is the perfect place to rest out of the sun, grab a cool moment of tranquillity, or enjoy a serene park-bench picnic. Here hundreds of intriguing plant varieties grow in profusion, set in a peaceful shady park of only 2.5ha. Almost everything in the gardens is a native of another land, the focal point being a huge 200-year-old fig tree, brought here as a sapling from South America. Today it rears up on an astonishing platform of roots. Like the other plants, it has truly flourished in these foreign soils, a testimony to the benign climate and conditions of the island.

The gardens were set up in 1788 by King Carlos III as part of an experiment to see if it was possible to acclimatise plants to live in other climate zones. The intention was to see if useful varieties from tropical colonies could survive elsewhere, for it was not known how or why plant species live only in certain parts of the globe. The correct name of the Jardín Botánico to this day is El Jardín de Aclimatación de La Orotava (La Orotava Acclimatisation Garden).

The range of species is prodigious, and includes several thousand plant varieties. Pepper trees, breadfruit trees, cinnamon trees and tulip trees mingle with coffee bushes and mango trees. Lovers of exotic flowers will be thrilled by the splendid hothouse orchids.

Tropical plants that thrived in these gardens were then taken to similar Royal Gardens at Madrid and Aranjuez in Spain to see whether – after their spell of adapting to the climate in Tenerife – they could 'learn' to survive on the mainland. For most, mainland Spain proved simply too cold in winter and the results were broadly unsuccessful.

INFORMATION

➕ C1
✉️ Calle Retama 2, off Carretera del Botánico
☎️ 922 383572
🕐 Summer: daily 9–7; Winter: 9–6
♿ Few
💰 Cheap
🍴 Hotel Botánico (£££); no casual dress
🚌 Carretera del Botánico

Reflect on the ornamental pond at the Jardín Botánico

29

Lago Martíanez

INFORMATION

➕ C1

✉ Playa Martíanez, Avenida de Colón

☎ 922 38 38 52

🕐 Daily 10–7 (last entry 5PM)

♿ Few

💲 Moderate

🍴 Several eating places on site (£–£££)

🚌 Along waterfront

↔ Ermita San Telmo (► 58)

As a traditional resort, Puerto de la Cruz had a major drawback in the new era of mass package tourism: it had no decent beach.

The solution was this beautiful lido, designed by the inspirational Lanzarote architect César Manrique and completed in 1977. Manrique was also responsible for the Playa Jardín, also in Puerto de la Cruz, which he developed in 1992 (► 55).

In the 1970s, when the town wondered how to respond to the growing demand for swimming and sunbathing, it consulted Manrique, who was based on Lanzarote. An acclaimed international modern artist, he had recently returned to his native Canaries, where he had been given a free hand to develop tourist attractions.

Manrique had strong views on mass tourism, which he believed could be of great benefit to the Canary Islands, but at the risk of destroying the landscape, local culture and traditional architecture. He argued that tourism should be encouraged within strict controls, and that facilities should be of the highest, most creative standard.

Marketed under various names (Costa Martíanez, Lido de San Telmo, Lido de Martíanez), the Lago contains some 27,000 cubic metres of filtered seawater. It consists of eight attractively shaped pools and a larger swimming lake, interspersed with refreshing fountains and islets of lush, colourful greenery; the complex has proved a great success. Waterside sunbathing terraces, shaded by palms, are laid out in white and black volcanic rock.

Touches of art and humour are everywhere; a popular feature is a central lava isle which periodically erupts as a fountain.

Loro Parque

The premier family attraction on Tenerife is a tropical wildlife park that mixes conservation, education, entertainment and fun.

This is one of the original tourist attractions on Tenerife, located in the island's first holiday resort. From simple beginnings in 1972 as a parrot park (which is what Loro Parque means), today it's an internationally acclaimed award-winning wildlife theme park, an extravaganza of tropical gardens, a dolphinarium and sea life centre with many related attractions and rides. Covering 12.5ha, with over 2,000 palm trees, it's home to a colony of gorillas, and has a water zone where the ever-popular sea lions and dolphins seem to relish their role as a holiday entertainment. The park's aquarium tunnel, believed to be the longest in the world, is a transparent underwater walkway 18.5m long. As you walk along, sharks slip through the water, just a few centimetres away. There are flamingos, crocodiles, cranes, giant turtles, jaguars, monkeys and a Nocturnal Bat Cave. A recent addition is Planet Penguin, claimed to be the biggest penguinarium in the world. A special effects cinema, Natura Vision, takes you on a trip through other wildlife centres around the world.

Parrots, however, remain an important element of the Park. There are over 300 species living here – the world's largest collection. The birds are being studied, and the park is engaged in important breeding and conservation work. While endangered parrot species may be confined, the more common varieties are used in parrot shows several times each day. These feature clever tricks and elaborate entertainments which the parrots have learned to perform.

INFORMATION

- C1
- 1.5km west of Puerto de la Cruz near Punta Brava
- 922 373841
- Daily 8:30–6:30 (last admission 5PM)
- Good
- Expensive
- Choice on site, including a pizzeria (££) and a self-service buffet (£)
- Free shuttle bus from Avenida de Colón (near Lido) and Plaza del Charco every 20 mins
- Puerto de la Cruz (➤ 30)

Lunch to go in the Loro Parque

31

Los Gigantes

INFORMATION

Los Gigantes

These stupendous sheer cliffs are called The Giants, an apt description of the rockface that soars 600m from blue sea to the blue sky.

One of Tenerife's most breathtaking sights is best seen from a boat: properly known as Acantilados de los Gigantes, the soaring dark rock face rising 600m from the Atlantic waves marks the abrupt edge of northwestern Tenerife's Teno Massif. There's nothing more to the site but its sheer grandeur, but that's enough to attract almost all visitors to Tenerife. Come by car or coach and join a sightseeing boat when you arrive, or, perhaps better, take a boat excursion from one of the resorts. Either way, it's not until you see another boat cruising gently at the foot of these cliffs that their true majesty becomes clear.

The cliffs rise from one end of a pleasant bay called La Canalita. At the other end of bay,

there's a small resort with a quiet, civilised feel and a black sand beach called Playa de los Guios. Being slightly remote, it preserves a calm holiday atmosphere now rare on the island. The cliffs and the sea guarantee that this little resort cannot expand much.

South of Los Gigantes, however, the coast has been heavily developed, mostly with apartment blocks. An excellent black sand beach called Playa de la Arena near the former fishing village of Puerto de Santiago creates a focal point to the suburban sprawl.

Mercado Nuestra Señora de África

Tenerife's main produce market, the market of Our Lady of Africa, is a dazzle of colour and energy, a picture of the island's abundance.

The generosity of the Canaries and their surrounding ocean, and their ready access to all the abundance of the rest of Spain, are apparent daily in the wonderful displays in this lively and atmospheric enclosed marketplace. Flowers fill the eye, alongside the colours of myriad fruits and vegetables. Other stalls are laden with fish and meat. You'll find small live animals, a multitude of curious peasant cheeses made of cows', sheep's or goats' milk (or sometimes all three) and home-made honey. Here too are the traders selling cheap cassettes and CDs – often of foot-stamping Spanish and Latin American music. Interestingly, all is neat and orderly, with a surprising tidiness and efficiency.

The market is located near the heart of the oldest quarter of Tenerife's capital town, not far from the lanes of a red-light district, and usually spills out into these surrounding streets, where stalls sell 'dry goods' – kitchenware, fabrics and household items. The market entrance itself is a circular arch, leading straight into the flower-stall area. Beyond lies a veritable bazaar of stalls within the central courtyard.

There's officially no market here on Sunday, but that's when the big weekly *rastro* sets up outside the market hall. A *rastro* is a mixed flea market and craft market, where an array of stallholders from home and abroad sell a hotch-potch of cheap souvenirs, second-rate factory-made 'craft' items, leather goods, assorted cast-offs and secondhand items, as well as plenty of genuine high-quality arts and crafts. Philatelists will love it: stamps are a particular speciality of several stallholders.

INFORMATION

☩ b2

✉ Just off Calle de San Sebastián, at the south end of Puente Servador, Santa Cruz

☎ 622 606090

🕐 Mon–Sat 8–1 (Sun *rastro* market 10–2)

♿ Few

↔ Santa Cruz (➤ 47)

❓ Watch out for pickpockets! Tourists at the market are seen as easy prey

Blooms for sale at the colourful Mercado de Nuestra Señora de África

Museo de Antropología de Tenerife

INFORMATION

➕ D1

✉ 44 Carretera
Tacoronte–Valle de
Guerra, 25km from
Puerto de la Cruz

☎ 922 150534

🕐 Tue–Sun 10–8

♿ Few

✋ Moderate (Sun free)

🍴 In and around nearby
Tacoronte (££)

🚌 Call Tacoronte Bus
Information ☎ 922
561807

*Traditional Canarian
country architecture*

A fascinating collection of Canary Islands folk culture, housed in a fine restored country mansion, one of the most beautiful buildings on the island.

This beautiful, low, white-painted Canarian farmhouse and country mansion dates back to the end of the 17th century, and is one of Tenerife's prettiest architectural gems. Faultlessly restored, the building is an exquisite arrangement of carved wooden doors, balconies, porticos and patios. It stands among tropical gardens in the countryside overlooking the village of Valle de Guerra.

For centuries the home of the Carta family of regional administrators, the building now houses the Tenerife Anthropology Museum. Reconstructed rooms reveal much about life in rural Tenerife, and there are examples of all the island's ancestral crafts and folk arts and crafts. Inside, 14 exhibition rooms with their galleries are used to re-create appealing little glimpses of ordinary life in the rural Tenerife of past times. The principal displays are of weaving, needlework and pottery, as well as farm tools, fabrics, clothing, ceramics and furniture.

The most interesting exhibits are of Canary Islands traditional dress from the 18th century onwards, highlighting the small but important differences of style and colour between one island and the next. Embroidered and patterned festival clothes, wedding clothes and everyday workwear are on show. The weaving and sewing rooms show how these clothes would have been made in the past.

Museo de Historia de Tenerife

To get a vivid overview of Tenerife's story since the arrival of the Spanish, linger at this excellent museum in the centre of historic La Laguna.

Anyone wanting to learn about Tenerife's heritage should visit the town of San Cristóbal de la Laguna, which is of exceptional importance to students of Canarian history. It is the ideal place for a museum of Tenerife's post-conquest culture and development.

As the first town of Tenerife and the first Spanish capital of the Canary Islands, the first bishopric in the Canaries, the first community in the archipelago to have a town hall, and also seat of the first university in the Canary Islands, La Laguna has a unique inheritance and has preserved many historic buildings. A fine example is Casa Lercaro on Calle San Augustin, a grandiose 16th–century colonial mansion, which provides the setting for the Museum of Tenerife History. The house itself, in an Italianate Genoese style incorporating a facade with Renaissance features, deserves a visit. Home of the aristocratic Lecaro family, it later served as part of the university.

Those wanting to understand the development of Tenerife under Spanish rule will likely wish to spend a couple of hours under the spell of this impressive treasure-house of archives and artefacts. High points of the collections include priceless historical maps of the Canaries, believed to be among the oldest in existence, as well as maritime exhibits, colonial documents, and artefacts concerning the administrative, military, cultural and economic development of the islands from the 15th century onwards.

INFORMATION

➕ F1

✉ Calle San Agustin 22, La Laguna

☎ 922 825949

🕐 Tue–Sun 9–8:30

♿ Few

💰 Cheap

The impressive carved balcony of the museum

Museo de la Ciencia y el Cosmos

INFORMATION

➕ E1

✉ Calle Vía Láctea, off the La Cuesta road, near the university, La Laguna

☎ 922 315265

🕐 Tue–Sun 9–8:30 (shorter hours in winter)

♿ Few

💵 Moderate (Sun free)

This fascinating and entertaining museum sets out to show the relationship between man and earth, within the universe.

With a variety of hands-on exhibits and displays, visitors to this imaginative astrophysics centre can enjoy a huge range of science. Housed inside a striking, modern building, the museum supports an 18–m radio telescope (painted with a full moon) on its roof. The interior is divided into five areas called the Sun, the Universe, the Earth, the Human Body and How Does It Work?

The different sections explore other galaxies, our own solar system and the human body, complete with such diversions as listening to the sound of a baby in the womb, taking a lie detector test and watching a skeleton ride a bicycle!

Recognising that not all visitors are scientists, the museum's approach skilfully blends a serious scientific attitude with the need to amuse and stimulate the visitor. Guided telescope tours include a session of sun-watching that gives a spectacular view of phenomena such as the solar chromosphere and the bulges on the sun's surface. Other activities include laboratory demonstrations and sessions in the separate planetarium and Virtual Reality area.

Astronomers, engineers and artists have created scores of interactive exhibits, set in the large elliptical central hall that represents the solar system. The hall is dominated by an image of the sun projected from a 'heliostat' on the roof. The section devoted to the earth looks closely at the climatic problems of global warming and the damaged ozone layer, as well as hurricanes, storms and other geological and meteorological phenomena. Not forgotten are volcanoes of Tenerife.

Museo de la Naturaleza y el Hombre

The landscape, life and death of ancient Canarians are explored in this Santa Cruz museum, including the mummies of the Guanche people.

INFORMATION

➕ b2
✉ Calle Fuentes Morales, Santa Cruz
☎ 922 209320
🕐 Tue–Sun 10–8
♿ Good
💶 Moderate (Sun free)
🍴 Nearby in Plaza de la Candelaria
🔁 Santa Cruz (➤ 47)

This worthy museum, situated in a most attractive former hospital with a galleried courtyard, deals seriously but accessibly with the archaeology, anthropology and ethnography of the Canary Islands, as well as the natural history.

The museum is essentially two museums in one – Nature and Man are dealt with separately – and is split in half following the plan of the building. The archaeology of the Canaries lies on the left of the entrance and the fauna and flora of the islands on the right. Ten distinct sections tackle these different aspects of the Canary Islands with displays as varied as African and pre-Columbian art, aboriginal therapy, the Canaries during the Spanish Conquest and the Canary Islands today.

The main emphasis is placed on the islands' pre-Hispanic history and culture. Much of the evidence of Guanche culture relates to burial, and the museum displays fascinating material on Guanche tombs and burial sites.

Dramatic exhibits include preserved bodies in a display on mummification, as well as skeletons and hundreds of skulls, some of them trepanned (drilled with holes). Interesting too, though less dramatic, are the displays of Guanche household items, pottery, tools and body decorations, as well as indigenous Canarian plant and animal life.

Welcome shelter in the museum's shaded courtyard

Basílica Nuestra Señora de la Candelaria

INFORMATION

✠ E2

✉ On the coast 17km south of Santa Cruz, Candelaria, Plaza de la Basílica

🕐 Daily 7:30–1, 3–7:30

♿ Few

💷 Free

🍴 Bars and restaurants in the town centre (£–£££)

🚌 122, 123, 124, 127, 131 from Santa Cruz

🔄 Santa Cruz (➤ 47)

❓ Festival of the Virgin 14–15 Aug (also celebrated throughout the Canaries)

The statue of the Virgin inside the church

The modern Basilica of Our Lady of Candelaria is dedicated to the revered patron saint of the Canary Islands – the Virgin of local legend

The Virgin is always depicted holding the child in her right arm and a candle in her left hand. Spiritually, her role is as the symbolic bringer of Christian light to the darkness of Guanche life, and so she represents the rightness and justice of the Spanish occupation of the islands.

The legend told by early Spanish settlers – not by the Guanches – was that over a century before the arrival of the first Spanish *conquistadores* the Guanches found a statue of the Virgin and Child set up in a seaside cave. A multitude of legends claim the statue worked miracles to prevent the Guanches from harming her, and that the overawed Guanches began to worship the figure, which they called Chaxiraxi. In a mix of fact and fancy, it is related that the *mencey* (chieftain) of the Guanches welcomed the Spanish at this spot, but that the Guanches were already Christians when the conquerors arrived.

The huge modern (1958) Basílica de Nuestra Señora de la Candelaria, set back from the sea, dominates the small town. Inside, the statue of the Virgin sits enthroned in a glorious gilt setting behind the altar, among immense devotional murals. The statue dates from about 1830, and what exactly became of the Guanches' Chaxiraxi (which may have looked quite different from today's Virgin) is the stuff of myth. Even before the Spanish arrived in Tenerife, a European living on Fuerteventura is said to have stolen the Guanche statue, but replaced it. Either the original, or its copy, was damaged by fire in 1789 and repaired or replaced. That statue was washed out to sea and completely lost in 1826, being replaced by the present version a few years later.

16

Nuestra Señora de la Concepción

When Guanche leaders were 'persuaded' to become Christian and submit to Spanish rule, this grandiose church was used for their baptisms.

The oldest church on the island, with much outstanding craftsmanship, Our Lady of the Immaculate Conception represents a landmark in Canarian history and has the status of a Spanish national shrine. Its greatest claim to fame is that the big glazed 16th-century baptismal font, brought here from Seville in southern Spain, was used to 'convert' defeated Guanche warriors to Christianity. You'll find it in the *baptisterio* (baptistery) set to one side of the main entrance, with family trees displayed above.

Though much changed since, even in those days the church was extraordinarily grand for a far-flung new colony, with elaborately carved gilded wooden ceiling panels in Moorish design. Over the centuries, the church benefited from the finest workmanship on the island, its Gothic origins becoming overlaid with Renaissance style and then gaudy baroque decoration.

First built in 1502, the triple-naved church has probably the grandest and richest interior on Tenerife, and rivals any other building in the Canaries. The gold and silver paintwork and metalwork are breathtaking, together with rich retables from the 17th century and later. Immediately obvious on entering the building, the extravagant woodcarving of the 18th-century pulpit is considered one of Spain's best examples of this type of work. The choir stalls, too, are beautifully carved.

The eye-catching seven-storey tower, dating from the 17th century, has a distinctive Moorish look and is the principal landmark of historic La Laguna.

INFORMATION

- E1
- Plaza de la Concepción, La Laguna
- Usually Mon–Fri 11–1, 5–8. Sat–Sun services only
- Few
- Cheap
- Tapas bars and restaurants nearby
- 102 (Puerto de la Cruz or Santa Cruz–La Laguna) every 30 mins

The gilded altar within Nuestra Señora de la Concepción.

Parque Marítimo César Manrique

INFORMATION

🔲 E1

✉ Avenida de la
Constitución, Santa Cruz

☎ 922 202995

🕐 Daily 10–7

♿ Good

💲 Moderate

🍴 Choice on site (£–£££)

🚌 909 and others along
Avenida de la
Constitución

🔄 Santa Cruz (➤ 47)

A beautiful shore-side haven of pools and palms, Parque Marítimo is a popular destinatation for a day splashing around and sunbathing.

When the Cabildo (Island Council) of Tenerife wanted to do something with the unsightly disused industrial dockyards near the old Castillo de San Juan, they commissioned the brilliant Canarian artist and designer César Manrique to create something for them.

Manrique belived that tourism would be the salvation of the Canary Islands if carefully controlled, but could ruin the islands if given free rein. At Santa Cruz his brief was limited, but even so Manrique managed to redesign the docklands site into an attractive leisure complex linking the sea with the Castillo.

The Castillo itself dates back to 1641, and was one part of the town's defences (the Castillo San Cristóbal was located where the Plaza de España lies now). It was once a marketplace for African slaves.

Today the César Manrique Marine Park is a delightful lido, with palms and terraces around a beautiful seawater pool (similar to the lido Manrique created for Puerto de la Cruz, ➤ 60).

To the east of the fort lies the town's new Auditorio. Designed like a sea-shell by Santiago Calatrava, it is Santa Cruz's main concert hall. Southwards stretches a huge palm park (Palmetum), still being planted, while across the busy coastal highway is a large, eye-catching exhibition space for trade fairs and conferences.

Lay back and relax at the lido

Parque Nacional de Garajonay, La Gomera

A vast area of protected Canarian forest covers the central upland of La Gomera: a strange, dark wilderness of lichens, ravines and laurel canyons.

While sun beats down on the southern shore, a cooler, damper climate prevails around Mount Garajonay. Heather, ferns and lichens flourish, creating a thick carpet across the boulders and rocky slopes where the last of the original Canarian laurel woodland survives. Waterfalls and streams splash through the greenery. Walking in this wet, magical terrain among the slender, sinuous limbs of the Canary laurel (*Larus canariensis*), it is certainly hard to believe that you are in the Canary Islands. Not just laurel but also the luxuriant Canary date palm (*Phoenix canariensis*) grows here in great numbers, and there are around 400 species of native flowers, some found only at this place. There are, too, many rare insects and birds.

A useful starting point if you are passing is the the Centro de Visitantes (Visitor Centre) at Juego de Bolas, on the north side of the forest. This gives an overview of the Park and its flora and fauna, and details all the marked forest walks. The centre has much else of interest about La Gomera, including gardens, a small museum, and displays about island life over the centuries. Craftspeople demonstrate traditional skills such as weaving, pottery, basketmaking and carpentry.

Easy, popular walks start at La Laguna Grande in the middle of the forest, where there's a small information centre, a play area, a board showing marked trails, and a track up to a lofty mirador (viewpoint).

INFORMATION

- ⊞ Inside front cover
- ⌖ None
- 🎟 Free
- 🍴 Restaurants at La Laguna (££)
- 🚌 Agulo (➤ 50), Chipude (➤ 50), Hermingua (➤ 51)

Centro de Visitantes

- ✉ Juego de Bolas, near Las Rosas (35km from San Sebastián)
- ☎ 922 800993
- 🕐 Tue–Sun 9:30–4:30. The craft workshops are open Tue–Fri only
- ⌖ Few
- 🎟 Free

Traditional hand-crafted Gomeran earthenware

Pico del Teide

INFORMATION

➕ C2

✉️ Parque Nacional del Teide

🍴 Nearest are the *parador* and at El Portillo

🚌 348 leaves Puerto de la Cruz at 9:15 and arrives at the *teleférico* at 11:15; return trip 4:15. Bus 342 leaves Playa de las Américas at 9:15 and arrives at the *teleférico* at 11:15; return trip 3:40. Bus times can be unreliable

♿ None

💷 Cable car expensive

❓ Permits to climb the last 163m from the cable-car station are restricted to 150 per day. Available from ✉️ National Park office, Calle Emilio Calzadilla 5, Santa Cruz 🕐 Mon–Fri 9–2 ☎️ 922 290129 All applicants require passports. Check the cable car and weather before starting

The highest mountain in all Spain is an active – but sleeping – volcano, soaring majestically above the Atlantic island it helped to create.

Pico del Teide was aflame as Christopher Columbus passed this way. The sailors took it for an ill omen, Columbus for a good one. Before the Spanish conquest, the Guanche people revered the mountain. The most recent eruption was a small one in 1898, and the volcano has been quiet since; it has made some noises of late and scientists are monitoring any risk.

Over the millennia, Pico del Teide's eruptions have added more and more land to the island of Tenerife, though the terrain all around the volcano is a blasted landscape of twisted rock and debris, a devastation that thrills and amazes visitors. This region now has protected status within the Parque Nacional del Teide (▶ 66). Although not an attraction, not an entertainment, not even particularly accessible, and offering nothing but its dignified presence, Pico del Teide ranks first among the 'must sees' of Tenerife.

Pico del Teide is a mere remnant of the original Tenerife volcano, the cone of which at some point blew itself to pieces in a massive eruption. The relics of the cone surround Pico del Teide in a ring of lesser volcanic outlets, which are known as the Caldera de las Cañadas.

The 3,718m mountain does not always permit people to visit, guarding itself in mist, snow or strong winds – even when the weather is perfect down on the coast. In the height of summer, heat can be a problem, often reaching 40°C. However, on fine, calm days the summit can be approached either on foot in around 3 hours or, more usual, by *teleférico* (cable car) in 8 minutes. The cable car can, however, involve long waits (over an hour is not unusual).

Playa de las Américas & Los Cristianos

Los Cristianos effectively merges with Playa de las Américas, though it's less brash, more family orientated and has some Spanish character.

The throbbing heart of Tenerife's package holiday scene is a round-the-clock resort with a vast choice of accommodation, bars, restaurants and entertainment. Surprisingly, the location is still beautiful, with rocky hills behind and attractions around the edges of town. The area extends westward from Los Cristianos through Playa de las Américas and into the newer district of Costa Adeje.

Los Cristianos was the only coastal town in the late 1960s. So when sun-seekers arrived in the south, it was to this harbour that they came. The town already had a few bars and a good natural beach, and owed its existence as a port to a sun-trap location well sheltered from the wind. Even with the subsequent massive growth, the town maintains its separate identity and a refreshing sense of reality which is sometimes lacking at the newer resort next door. The focal point is the bustling harbour area, from where ferries depart for La Gomera.

Playa de las Américas – love it or hate it, you should see it. Look out for the restaurant signs that boast, 'No Spanish food served here!' One of the most successful purpose-built resorts in the world, Playa de las Américas started construction at the end of the 1960s and has become almost a byword for how not to develop tourism. Unfocused, sprawling, much of it frankly ugly, it nevertheless rightly remains supremely popular for a fun-and-sun holiday. The beaches have been greatly improved, the weather is perfect, and for those who want to start the day with a full English breakfast at lunchtime, swim and tan all afternoon, and dance all night, this is the place.

INFORMATION

- B3
- Autopista del Sur exits 27, 28, 29 or 30
- Tourist restaurants (£–££) near beaches and close to Puerto Colón and Los Cristianos harbour
- 111 to Santa Cruz. Frequent services to all southern resorts. TITSA information ☎ 922 531300
- Centro Commercial, Playa de las Américas ☎ 922 797668. Centro Commercial, Plaza del Carmen, Los Christianos ☎ 922 757137

The bright lights of Playa de las Américas

Playa de las Teresitas

+ F1
- San Andrés, 8km north of Santa Cruz
- Bars and fish restaurants in San Andrés (£–££)
- 910 from Santa Cruz; 246 (Santa Cruz–Almaciga) stops 3 or 4 times daily
- Few
- Santa Cruz (➤ 47)

On the beach at Las Teresitas

Popular and usually lively, Las Teresitas is a beautiful golden beach in a large bay with an offshore breakwater for protection.

Despite its huge popularity, the appeal of Tenerife pre-dates the sun, sea and sand recipe of mass tourism. Most beaches are unattractive and made of rough, dark volcanic material (which comes as a shock to some visitors). However, island authorities are aware of the lack and have created some artificial beaches.

By far the most outstanding of these is the beautiful curve of Las Teresitas, created in the 1970s with 98,000 cubic metres of sand from the Sahara desert. Ironically, it was created not in the tourist heartland of the south, but in the north, where locals could enjoy it. Nude sunbathing occurs at Playa de las Gaviotas, further north. San Andrés, at the southwest end of the beach, is a working fishing village with a choice of restaurants. From here the rising Anaga Mountains can be explored (➤ 58, 51).

Plaza del Adelantado

The secret of La Laguna is its exquisite historic quarter, where many fine 16th- and 17th-century Renaissance mansions survive.

The heart of old La Laguna is a pleasant, shaded square where locals relax on benches enclosed by some of the most striking historic and dignified civic buildings in town, including the Ayuntamiento and the Santa Catalina church – as well as beautiful mansions adorned with fine porches and balconies. There are bars here too, and the town's busy Mercado Municipal (main market), with its lattice gallery, is the place to join locals in the morning stocking up with fruit and vegetables.

At the start of Calle Obispo Rey Redondo, La Laguna's town hall or *ayuntamiento* is a charming building in Tenerife style. Originally constructed in the 16th century, it was rebuilt in 1822 with fine wooden panelling, and a Moorish-style window. Inside, murals illustrate key events in the island's past, and the flag Alonso Fernández de Lugo placed on Tenerife soil has been displayed here.

Next door, Casa de los Capitánes Generales (House of the Captain Generals) is the impressive residence of the island's military commanders, built in 1624. Today it is used as a temporary exhibition space.

The latticework gallery of the Santa Catalina Convent Church, beside the town hall, is one of several attractive architectural features. Inside, the former convent church has a silver-covered altar and baroque *retablos*. Notice the little revolving hatch near the side entrance in Calle Dean Palahi, used by mothers who once wished to abandon their newborn girl babies by 'donating' them anonymously to the convent, to be brought up as nuns.

INFORMATION

➕ E1
✉️ Mercado Municipal, Plaza del Adelantado, La Laguna
☎️ 922 258774
🕐 Mon–Sat 8–1
🍴 Bars with *tapas* around the square (£)

Traditional street architecture in Plaza del Concepción

San Sebastián de La Gomera

INFORMATION

➕ Inside front cover

✉ On east coast of island

ℹ Calle Real 4

☎ 922 141512

🍽 Inexpensive bars in town
(£), and the best food on
the island at the *parador*
(£££)

🚌 The intermittent bus
service is not reliable.
Taxis are readily available
at the ferry dock

🔁 Parque Nacional de
Garajonay (➤ 41)

❓ Local saint's festival
around 20 Jan

Pozo de la Aguada

✉ Calle Real

☎ 922 141512

🕐 Mon–Sat 9–1:30, 3:30–6,
Sun 10–1

♿ None

💷 Free

❓ Located in the same
building as the tourist
office

Iglesia de NS de la Asunción

✉ Calle Real

♿ None

💷 Free

Casa de Colón

✉ Calle Real 56

☎ 922 870155

🕐 Mon–Fri 9–1, 4:30–7:30,
Sat 9–1

♿ None

💷 Free

La Gomera was the last Canary Island to be subjugated by the Spanish – in fact it remained independent right into the 19th century.

No other Canary Island retains so much of the native Guanche culture and ethnicity. There are, too, visible in many island faces, reminders of the many African slaves who were kept here. When Christopher Columbus anchored at San Sebastián before the journey that discovered the Americas, this was the most westerly port in the world. Tenerife remained in Guanche hands, while on La Gomera only this edge of the island was under Spanish control.

To recapture a little of that past, walk along the main street, Calle Real. Here is the 17th-century Casa del Pozo, once the customs house; the name means House of the Well. Inside is the Pozo de la Aguada, the well from which Columbus's quartermaster drew the water to supply his ships on the outward voyage to America. Here too the expedition bought seeds, grains and flowers.

In the same street stands the Iglesia Nuestra Señora de la Asunción (Church of Our Lady of the Assumption; rebuilt in the 18th century), where – allegedly – Columbus said his last prayer before setting out on the great voyage.

Also in Calle Real is Casa de Colón (Columbus House), claimed as the house where he lodged. It has been restored as a museum about Columbus and is the focal point of the annual Columbus Festival in September.

Finally, in the harbourside park, the Torre del Conde (Count's Tower, closed to visitors) is the oldest building in continuous use in the Canary Islands. This sturdy brick tower house dates from 1447, and during its most famous era was the residence of Countess Beatriz de Bobadilla (➤ 9).

Santa Cruz de Tenerife

During the five centuries since the conquest, Santa Cruz has remained the focal point of Tenerife's culture and history.

INFORMATION

⊞ E1

🛈 Palacio Insular (ground floor), Plaza de Espana
☎ 922 239592
🕐 Mon–Fri 8–6, Sat 9–1

Santa Cruz, the island's capital, still has the authentic feel and look of colonial Spain. It's not a holiday resort, but a vibrant Latin city where most Tinerfeños live and work. The name means Holy Cross of Tenerife, and comes from the crucifix planted boldly at this spot by the ruthless Spanish conqueror Alonso Fernández de Lugo, when he strode ashore in 1493 with 1,000 men to take possession of the Guanches' island home.

While the gaudy, multicultural Tenerife of modern tourism stays way down south, the resolutely Spanish capital has remained almost unaffected by the millions of package holiday visitors.

Only tourists determined to know and understand the island, and looking for something more than a suntan, choose to stay here. This is partly due to the climate: most of the island's scant rain falls on this stretch of the coast. It's also due to the diverse economy of the capital, with its oil processing, water-front industry and deep-water harbour.

Now though, Santa Cruz has polished up some of its treasures and even provides a jaunty little 'train' to take people on a tour of the sights. At the same time, holidaymakers have realised there's more to Tenerife than just sunbathing, and that much of the best sightseeing is in and around Santa Cruz. The redeveloped waterfront area with its diverse shipping continues to be a source of interest, while just north of the city lies a little-know treasure, the best beach on Tenerife.

City life in Santa Cruz

47

Valle Gran Rey, La Gomera

INFORMATION

A sculpture by César Manrique, set on a cairn in Valle Gran Rey

Offering sea, sand, views and lush plantations, it's not surprising this splendid valley is no longer a well-kept secret.

On the west side of the island, the majestic Valley of the Great King is still remote and was almost unknown until the 1970s. Then it was a retreat for various Greens and hippies – offering an away-from-it-all, ecologically sustainable lifestyle. Today, though, and despite the location, it attracts more visitors than anywhere else on the island.

On the twisting road up to Arure (10km inland), several viewpoints offer stunning panoramas of cultivated terraces clinging to the lower slopes of the steep ravine, the scattered white houses of a few hamlets, and the valley opening out to greenery beside the dazzling blue sea. One hamlet has a spectacularly located *mirador* restaurant designed by César Manrique.

The road descends to reach La Calera, the attractive little central community of the Valle Gran Rey, standing among banana plantations. Beyond, the road divides for the last 1km to the sea: north to La Playa; south to the fishing harbour and port at Vueltas, the traditional gateway to the valley. Both settlements have simple waterside eateries offering the freshest of fish. La Playa and Vueltas have developed as tourist centres since the 1980s and their little shingle beaches are among the best that La Gomera offers.

TENERIFE's
best

Towns & Villages

TRADE WINDS

On Tenerife and La Gomera, the northerly trade winds – known as *los alisios* – bring settled weather of rainfree days with some cloud. On the north or west of the islands, the wind can be troublesome, and cloud cover excessive. In the south, it means perfect holiday weather.

Grand design at Adeje

Having fun at Bajamar.

In the Top 25

🇹 LA OROTAVA (▶ 25)
🇹 GARACHICO (▶ 27)
🇹 ICOD DE LOS VINOS (▶ 28)
🇹 PLAYA DE LAS AMÉRICAS & LOS CRISTIANOS (▶ 43)
🇹 SANTA CRUZ (▶ 47)

ADEJE

One of the few places in southern Tenerife with a natural water supply, this unspoiled little southern hilltown is the starting point for walks to the Barranco del Infierno. Though quite unremarkable now, it was once a Guanche tribal settlement and later became the Tenerife base of the counts of Gomera, who had plantations here worked by 1,000 African slaves. Ruins of the counts' fortress, Casa Fuerte, can be seen, and there's a 16th-century church, Iglesia de Santa Ursula.

🟦 B3 ✉ 6km north from Playa de las Américas 🍴 Otelo I (££) by entrance to Barranco del Infierno 🚌 416 (Granadilla–Guía de Isora) and 441 (Los Cristianos–La Caleta) run via Playa de las Américas to Adeje every 30 mins

AGULO, LA GOMERA

A pearl of a village in a delightful setting above the northeast coast of La Gomera, Agulo is enclosed by steep green hills, pouring with waterfalls and streams after rain showers. The town's narrow cobbled streets are focused on a domed Moorish-looking church, while out to sea the inspiring vision of Pico del Teide rises from the clouds.

🟦 IFC ✉ 27km from San Sebastián on the northern road 🍴 Las Rosas (££) in Las Rosas hamlet, 2km west ↔ Hermigua (▶ below) ❓ Fiesta de San Marcos 25 Apr; Los Piques mid–late Jun (*silbo* language)

BAJAMAR

Bajamar makes a sharp contrast with the glitzier resorts on the south coast of Tenerife and has a loyal following. Once a fishing village, Bajamar has few signs of its past, and now seems unfocused, with a long promenade and side turns, with many bars, restaurants and shops. Here, on the extreme northern shores, constant breezes and turbulent currents stir up the waves onto the black beach.

🟦 B3 ✉ 15km northwest of La Laguna 🍴 Variety of bars and restaurants (£–££) 🚌 105 (Santa Cruz–Bajamar) every 30 mins

CHIPUDE, LA GOMERA

Chipude was until recently a simple, rustic hamlet high in the green heart of La Gomera. Among Gomerans its name used to be synonymous with a rustic way of life and poverty, and locals will say that the people of Chipude used to drive away intruders with stones. While better roads and communications have changed all that, the villagers still preserve their old customs and traditions, and it is here that you may hear *silbo* – not being demonstrated for tourists, but used to call to friends or neighbours

✚ IFC ✉ 29km west from San Sebastián, off the central highland routes 🍴 Village bars (£) 🔁 Parque Nacional de Garajonay (➤ 41)

GÜÍMAR

On the border between the green north and the dry south of Tenerife, Güímar lacks charm but is an authentic Tenerife community with few tourists. Up the slope behind the town stand six curious large mounds, the enigmatic Tenerife step pyramids.

✚ D2 ✉ About 23km southwest of Santa Cruz, and 3km inland from the coastal highway 🍴 Bars in Güímar (£) 🚌 120 from Santa Cruz every 30 minutes 🔁 Candelaria (➤ 38) ❓ Popular carnival first week of Feb; ancient midsummer festival in Jun

Pyrámides de Güímar Parque Etnográfico ✉ Calle Chacona ☎ 922 514510 🕐 Daily 9.30–6 ♿ Good 💷 Expensive

HERMIGUA, LA GOMERA

Lying in La Gomera's most fertile and productive valley, Hermigua threads along the road through its plantations of banana palms. It is a tiny, tranquil place, a stopping point for visitors who want to see local crafts being made and the interesting Los Telares *artesanía* (craft centre). Opposite is the 16th-century Convento de Santo Domingo.

✚ IFC ✉ 20km from San Sebastián on the northern road 🍴 El Silbo (£), a typical simple bar-restaurant in the village 🔁 Agulo (➤ 50)

The craft of the loom in the Los Telares artesanía, Hermigua.

LOS ABRIGOS

Located on the southeast coast of Tenerife, Los Abrigos is a fishing village noted for a multitude of first-rate little waterfront fish restaurants and has two beaches. Behind the village the Golf del Sur development includes an excellent golf course.

✚ C3 ✉ 3km from Autopista del Sur Exit 24 🍴 Along Paseo Maritimo (£–££)

VALLEHERMOSO, LA GOMERA

An attractive village – one of La Gomera's largest communities – Vallehermoso is indeed in a 'beautiful valley' as its name suggests. It is surrounded by forest, vineyards and palm plantations of date and banana. A striking 650m-high volcanic pinnacle close by is called Roque Cano, Dog Rock, supposedly for its resemblance to a canine tooth.

✚ IFC ✉ 48km northwest of San Sebastián 🍴 Simple bar-restaurants in the village centre (£)

Sculpture in Vallehermoso

51

Museums

In the Top 25

Ⅺ MUSEO DE ANTROPOLOGÍA (▶ 34)
Ⅻ MUSEO DE HISTORICA DE TENERIFE (▶ 35)
⅓ MUSEO DE LA CIENCIA Y EL COSMOS (▶ 36)
⅔ MUSEO DE LA NATURALEZA Y EL HOMBRE (▶ 37)

MUSEO ARQUEOLÓGICO

Located near the old fishing harbour, the Archaeological Museum is housed in an attractive 19th-century building. The collection relates to the ethnography of the Guanche people. Permanent displays include early maps, ceramics, equipment used in farming, jewellery, weapons and information on mummification. The museum hosts temporary exhibitions.

🚩 C1 ✉ Calle del Lomo, Puerto de la Cruz ☎ 922 371465 🕐 Tue–Sat 10–1, 5–9, Sun 10–1 ♿ Few 🖐 Inexpensive 🍴 Eating places nearby (£), especially in Calle de San Felipe

MUSEO DE LAS CIENCIAS NATURALES

A small museum with displays of local flora, fauna and history. There are pictures showing the route the lava took when Volcan Negra erupted into life over Garachico.

🚩 B2 ✉ Convento de San Francisco, Glorieta de San Francisco, Garachico 🕐 Mon–Fri 9–7, Sat 9–6, Sun, hols 9–2 ♿ None 🖐 Moderate

MUSEO MILITAR REGIONAL DE CANARIAS

Todo por la Patria – All for the Fatherland – is the inscription above the gateway into this collection of important relics from the military past of the Canary Islands. Housed in part of the semicircular 19th-century barracks, Cuartel de Almeida, the museum is proud and patriotic in tone.

✉ Calle San Isidro 2, Santa Cruz ☎ 922 271658 🕐 Tue–Sun 10–2 ♿ Few 🖐 Free 🚌 Santa Cruz (▶ 47) ❓ Remember to take your passport to the Muséo Militar – you probably won't be admitted without it!

MUSEO MUNICIPAL DE BELLAS ARTES

Together with the city library, the Municipal Fine Arts Museum is housed in a former Franciscan monastery. Inside, the collection on two storeys includes the work of Canarian artists, several of historical interest, and more distinguished European works mainly covering the 17th–19th centuries. Most interesting are the successive temporary exhibitions of art works loaned by Spain's leading museums.

🚩 b1 ✉ Calle José Murphy 12, Plaza del Príncipe, Santa Cruz ☎ 922 244358 🕐 Mon–Fri 10–8 ♿ Few 🖐 Free 🍴 Café del Príncipe (££) 🚌 Santa Cruz (▶ 47)

The founder of the Museo Municipal de Bellas Artes

Churches

CATEDRAL

La Laguna's large cathedral is older than it appears.
Founded in 1515, it was subsequently enlarged and a
neoclassical façade was added in 1813. This last
feature survives but the remainder was radically
rebuilt during the early 20th century.
➕ E1 ✉ Plaza de la Catedral, La Laguna ⏰ Mon–Sat 8–1, 5–7 30;
Sun open for Mass only 💷 Froo

IGLESIA CONVENTO SANTA CATALINA

The latticework gallery of the Santa Catalina Conven
Church, beside the town hall, is one of several
attractive architectural features. Inside, the former
convent church has baroque *retablos*.
➕ E1 ✉ Plaza del Adelantado, La Laguna ⏰ Mon–Sat 7–11:45,
Sun 6:30–8 💷 Free 🍴 In Plaza del Adelantado (£)

IGLESIA DE NUESTRA SEÑORA DE LA
CONCEPCIÓN

One of Santa Cruz's most important landmarks, this
church is also one of the city's most significant
historical monuments. Begun in 1502, much changed
in the 17th and 18th centuries, the church was
reopened in 1999 after being closed for restoration.
➕ c2 ✉ Plaza de la Iglesia, Santa Cruz ⏰ Daily 9–1, 5:30–8
♿ None 💷 Free 🍴 Nearby in Plaza de la Candelaria (££)
🔄 Santa Cruz (➤ 47)

IGLESIA DE NUESTRA SEÑORA DE LA PEÑA
DE FRANCIA

The Church of Our Lady of the Rock of France was
started in the 1680s and took nearly 20 years to
complete – the bell tower was only added some 200
years later. The baroque interior includes an ornate
altarpiece by Luis de la Cruz in a side chapel.
➕ C1 ✉ Plaza de la Iglesia, Puerto de la Cruz ☎ 922 380051
⏰ Mon–Sat 3–7, Sun 9–7; Mass daily 8:30, 6:30, 7 💷 Free
🍴 Drink or snack on terrace of Hotel Marquesa, Calle Quintana 11 (££)

IGLESIA DE SAN FRANCISCO

This delightful church was begun in 1680. Striking
features are the wooden ceiling, the painted arch, a
fine organ and two baroque *retablos* (altarpieces)
dating from the 17th and 18th centuries.
➕ b1 ✉ Calle Villalba Hervás, Santa Cruz ⏰ Mon–Fri 9–1, 5:30–8
♿ None 💷 Free 🍴 Café del Príncipe (£–££) in Plaza del Príncipe
🔄 Santa Cruz (➤ 47)

Green Spaces

ANAGA VIEWS

Most accessible of the Anaga viewpoints is Mirador de Jardina, near La Laguna. Much higher is Mirador Cruz del Carmen (920m), which gives a view of both coasts. Here stands a lonely 17th–century chapel, the Ermita Cruz del Carmen. Alongside there is a restaurant, and an information centre on the Parque Rural de Anaga. A short distance farther along the road, on the slope of Taborno, Mirador Pico del Inglés (992m) is the highest viewpoint. Nearer the northern tip of the range, Mirador del Bailadero (759m) gives a lofty view onto the village of Taganana.

JARDINES DEL ATLÁNTICO BANANERA

Though a second best to Bananera El Guanche (➤ 24), this is an opportunity to see, taste and learn about bananas in a genuine banana farm. You'll also learn lots of other things about Tenerife, including its crops and wild plants, and how Pico del Teide distributes the rainwater that falls on the island. There are guided tours round the gardens.

➕ C3 ✉ Autopista del Sur Exit 26, 5km northeast of Los Cristianos ☎ 922 720360 🕐 Daily 10–6, last admission 4:15 🚻 Expensive 🍴 On site (££) 🚌 Free from southern resorts

LAS MONTAÑAS DE ANAGA

Tenerife's northern range of soaring, wild mountains remains remarkably unspoiled and makes an ideal region for rambling and exploring well off the beaten track. Narrow, twisting roads give access to dramatic landscapes, while for walkers it is still possible to see villages reached only on rough tracks.

➕ F1 ✉ North of La Laguna 🍴 Mirador Cruz del Carmen (££) 🚌 245, 246, 247 from Santa Cruz

Keep your distance at the Parques Exóticos.

PARQUES EXÓTICOS

An astonishing sight in the barren terrain, this lush tropical garden is truly exotic. The main attraction is Amazonia, a slice of tropical rainforest inside a climatically controlled domed area. Parrots, hummingbirds and 5,000 butterflies fly freely around.

➕ C3 ✉ Autopista del Sur Exit 26, 3.5km northeast of Los Cristianos ☎ 922 795424 🕐 Daily 10–6 ♿ Few 🚻 Moderate 🍴 Restaurant on site (££) 🚌 Free shuttle bus from Los Cristianos

VILAFLOR

Quite unlike other settlements in the south, the 'Flower Town' is the highest village in the Canary Islands. Standing at 1,160m, it rises through cultivated terraces to pine forest on the volcanic slopes of Tenerife's Teide National Park.

➕ C3 ✉ On C821, 23km northeast of Los Cristianos 🍴 El Sombrerito (££) 🚌 342 from Playa de las Américas; 474 from Granadilla; 482 from Los Cristianos ⬌ Pico del Teide (➤ 42)

Beaches

EL MÉDANO

A near-constant breeze has been both the blessing
and the bane of Tenerife. El Médano, on the island's
exposed southeast corner, has the best natural
beaches, but if generally too windy for sunbathing to
be enjoyable, it is the leading resort for windsurfing.
➕ C3 ✉ Autopista del Sur Exit 22, 22km east from Los Cristianos
♿ Few 🍴 Bars and restaurants on waterfront (£–££) 🚌 470 and
other buses, Playa de las Américas–El Médano 🔁 Los Cristianos
(➤ 43)

*Windsurfing off El
Médano.*

LA PLAYA CALERA, LA GOMERA

The small shingle beach at this tourist centre is one
of the best that La Gomera can offer. Waterside bars
and restaurants serve fresh fish. There is another
beach at the harbour of Vueltas, 2km southeast.
➕ IFC ✉ 4km from Valle Gran Rey, La Gomera 🍴 Simple bars and
fish restaurants on the coast (£) 🚌 Occasional buses and boats from
San Sebastián 🔁 Valle Gran Rey (➤ 48)

PLAYA JARDÍN

In 1992 the Canarian artist César
Manrique transformed the rocky bay
near the Castillo de San Felipe into a
remarkable waterfront beach garden.
The site was chosen partly because
the coast is more sheltered here and
has less dangerous currents.
Imported dark sand forms a glorious
stretch of beach, heightened by
magnificent gardens of flowering
bushes, palms and exotics.
➕ C1 ✉ At the western end of Puerto de la
Cruz, near Punta Brava ♿ Few 🎫 Free 🍴 In
the nearby fishermen's quarter, especially Calle
San Felipe (£–££) 🚌 102, 325, 343, 382 from
Puerto de la Cruz 🔁 Lago Martiánez (➤ 30)

*Playa Jardín at Puerto de
la Cruz.*

PLAYA DE SANTIAGO, LA GOMERA

High on the cliffs above the stony beach stands the
delightful Hotel Jardín Tecina. Below the hotel, the
former fishing village is steadily expanding with bars
and restaurants.
➕ IFC ✉ Southerly point of La Gomera, 30km southwest from San
Sebastián 🍴 Simple places on the waterfront (£–££), Hotel Tecina (££)
🔁 Parque Nacional de Garajonay (➤ 41)

For Children

The island provides little that is especially for children, but it doesn't need to – most of Tenerife's attractions are a are a big hit with people of all ages.

AMAZING PLANTS
Plant life in Tenerife is not just of interest to gardeners – some of it is weird enough even to grab the attention of children.

BANANERA EL GUANCHE (➤ 24)
All about bananas – and other plants.
✉ 2km from Puerto de la Cruz, on road to La Orotava ☎ 922 331853 ⏰ Daily 9–6

DRAGO MILENARIO (➤ 26)
One of the largest and oldest specimens of this curious species.
✉ Icod de los Vinos 🚌 354, 363 from Puerto de la Cruz

JARDÍN BOTÁNICO (➤ 29)
Spot the giant South American fig tree in this exotic garden.
✉ Calle Retama 2, off Carretara del Botánico, Puerto de la Cruz ⏰ Summer, daily 9–7; winter, 9–6

JARDINES DEL ATLÁNTICO BANANERA
Another chance to go bananas at these lush gardens on Tenrife's south coast.
✉ Autopista del Sur Exit 26 ☎ 922 720403 ⏰ Tours at 10, 11:30, 1, 2:15 and 3:30

PARQUE NACIONAL DE GARAJONAY (➤ 41)
The twisting branches of the forest are like scenes from a movie.
✉ La Gomera

Animal Parks
LORO PARQUE (➤ 31)
A tropical wonderland of animals and birds, including performing dolphins, parrots, gorillas, tigers, monkeys, penguins and flamingos .
✉ 1.5km west of Puerto de la Cruz, near Punta Brava ☎ 922 373841 ⏰ Daily 8:30–5 🚌 Free shuttle from Avenida de Colón (near Lago) and Plaza del Charco, Puerto de la Cruz

PARQUE ECOLÓGICO AGUILAS DEL TEIDE
See condors and crocodiles, tigers, eagles and penguins in this dramatic tropical park, where in five display areas creatures put on regular performances. Also dodgem boats and other amusements.
🚏 B3 ✉ On Arona road 3km from Los Cristianos ☎ 922 753001 ⏰ Summer: daily 9–6; Winter: 10–6 🚌 Free shuttle bus from Playa de las Américas and Los Cristianos

On the perch in Loro Parque.

PARQUES EXÓTICOS
Cactus and animal park (▶ 54).
✚ C3 ✉ Autopista del Sur Exit 26 ☎ 922 795424 ⏰ Daily 10–6
🚌 Free shuttle bus from Los Cristianos

TENERIFE ZOO
Apes, lions, crocodiles and many other creatures.
✚ C3 ✉ Llano Azul, Arona (Autopista del Sur Exit 26) ☎ 922
790720 ⏰ Daily 9:30–6 🚌 Free shuttle bus from southern resorts

Camel Rides
CAMEL PARK
A farm in the sun, making wine, growing crops,
selling island crafts and offering camel excursions.
✚ B3 ✉ Autopista del Sur Exit 27 ☎ 922 721080 ⏰ Daily 10–5
🚌 Free shuttle bus from Playa de las Américas and Los Cristianos

CAMELLO CENTER
Hold on tight for camel rides and donkey safaris at El
Tanque. Afterwards have tea in an Arab tent.
✚ B2 ✉ El Tanque (east of Garachico) ☎ 922 136399 ⏰ Daily
10–6

Eating Out
Children are welcome in bars and restaurants.
However, restaurants, bars and cafés do not generally
list children's menus; instead, children are given
small portions of whatever they fancy.

Fiesta Magic
Come to Tenerife during the Santa Cruz carnival
(early to mid-Feb) for a wild week of mayhem and
all-night revelry that will thrill older children (though
might not appeal to younger ones). Otherwise, find a
fiesta during your visit for unforgettable memories.

Meeting Whales and Dolphins
Whale- and dolphin-watching is one of the most
popular activities on Tenerife. About 20 different
species of sea mammals live in Canary Island waters,
mostly off the west coast of Tenerife between Los
Cristianos and Los Gigantes. Glass-bottomed boats
offer a chance to spot other marine life too (▶ 79).

Under the Sea
YELLOW SUBMARINE
A submarine adventure exploring the sea.
✚ B3 ✉ South Pier, Puerto Colón, Playa de las Américas ☎ 922
715080 ⏰ Hourly trips 10–4 🚌 Free shuttle bus from southern
resorts and Aquapark

Water Fun
AQUAPARK
Slides, pools, dolphin shows and water features – plan
to spend at least half a day.
✚ B3 ✉ Autopista del Sur Exit 29, 2km north of Playa de las
Américas ☎ 922 7152 66 ⏰ Daily 10–6 🚌 Free shuttle bus
from southern resorts

ON FILM

Teide National Park (▶ 42) is
a good choice for a day out
with aspiring young movie
buffs. Intended to convey a
primeval wilderness, it has
featured as a background in
The Ten Commandments and
Planet of the Apes. In the film
One Million Years BC, Raquel
Welch appeared here wearing
only a fur bikini.

Water fun at Aquapark

*All aboard the Yellow
Submarine*

Free Attractions

Calle de San Agustín, La Laguna

Our Lady of Candelaria, in Plaza de Candelaria, Santa Cruz

CALLE SAN AGUSTÍN

In this delightful old-fashioned street parallel to Obispo Rey Redondo, look out for the Instituto de Canarias Cabrera Pinto (Cabrera Pinto Institute of Canarian Studies), noted for its exquisite traditional patio and handsome bell tower. The fine 17th-century façade next door, of the San Agustín monastery, is an empty shell – the building was destroyed by fire nearly 100 years ago.

➕ E1 ✉ Calle San Agustin, La Laguna 🍽 In Plaza del Adelantado (£)

ERMITA DE SAN TELMO (SAN TELMO HERMITAGE)

San Telmo (St Elmo) is the patron saint of sailors, and the seafarers of Puerto de la Cruz erected this simple waterfront chapel in his honour in 1626 (rebuilt in 1780 after a fire). Dazzling white but for a tiny bell tower, it is exquisitely pretty, and stands in a lovely little garden surrounded by the noisy ebb and flow of tourists and traffic.

➕ C1 ✉ Calle de San Telmo, Puerto de la Cruz 🕐 Daily. Services Wed, Sat 6 30PM, Sun 9 30, 11AM 🍽 Nearby (£–££)

PARQUE MUNICIPAL GARCÍA SANABRIA

This delightful 6-hectare park full of shrubs, trees, exotic flowers, fountains and tranquil corners is the largest – and probably the most beautiful – urban park in the Canary Islands. There is also a zoo and a play area.

✉ Off Rambla del General Franco, Santa Cruz ♿ Few 🍽 Snacks available at park kiosks (£) 🚌 Town buses along Rambla del General Franco

PLAZA DE LA CANDELARIA

This pleasant traffic-free square has good bars and shops, including an *artesanía* (craft shop). Centuries ago, it was the entrance to the vanished Castillo San Cristóbal. Today, the centrepiece of the plaza is the appealing baroque statue of *Our Lady of Candelaria*, holding the infant Jesus and a tall candle. Formerly known as Plaza del Castillo, the square acquired its new name along with the statue.

➕ c2 ✉ West of Plaza de España, Santa Cruz 🍴 Several bars and cafés in the square (£–££)

PLAZA DEL CHARCO

A *charco* is a pool or pond, and this animated raised square stands where once shallow waters collected from the sea and locals fished for shrimps. Now the plaza, with its ancient Indian laurel trees, is the very heart of Puerto's old quarter and full of life – with bars and cafés, buskers and strollers.

➕ C1 ✉ Off Calle Blanco, near the fishing harbour, Puerto de la Cruz 🍴 Several bars and restaurants in the square (£–££)

PLAZA DE ESPAÑA

A large square near the waterfront, this spacious plaza is the heart of the city. The huge central Monumento de los Caidos, Monument to the Fallen, honours local people who fell in war, including the Spanish Civil War – Franco's manifesto was broadcast from here. The monument is flanked by statues of two *menceys* (chieftains).

➕ c2 ✉ Off Avenida de José Antonio Primo de Rivera, Santa Cruz 🍴 Bars and cafés nearby (£–££)

PUERTO PESQUERO

There's no more picturesque reminder that Puerto does not exist only for tourists than this small working fishing harbour, not far from lively Plaza del Charco. A low harbour wall of volcanic stone encloses the little bay. Modest but brightly painted rowing boats are hauled up on the shore, where local men and boys gather to talk or work.

On one corner, beside the water, a handsome building of dazzling white paint and bare black stone is the former Casa de la Real Aduana – the Royal Customs House. Built in 1620, this small public office continued to function as a customs house right up until 1833. (It is not open to the public.) Behind are 18th-century harbour defences which protected the town and port from raiders.

Across the street, Casa de Miranda dates from 1730. It's a fine restored house, once the home of Venezuelan liberator Francisco Miranda, and now a bar and restaurant.

➕ C1 ✉ At the end of Calle Blanco, Puerto de la Cruz 🍴 In Calle Blanco and Plaza del Charco (£–££)

Places to Have Lunch

Lunch alfresco in the shade

CASA DEL VINO, LA BARANDA (££)
Enjoy excellent tapas and island wines on the terrace of this delightful 17th-century country house.
✉ Autopista del Norte, km 21 (El Sauzal) ☎ 922 572535

CHEZ ARLETTE (£)
Spectacular views over the Masca gorge make this simple place ever-popular with visitors to the Teno Massif in northwest Tenerife.
✉ La Piedra, Masca ☎ 922 863459

EL MONASTERIO (££)
In the hilly countryside behind Puerto de la Cruz, this charming place is set in a former convent. Rustic dining rooms leading to sunny terraces beyond.
✉ La Montañeta, Los Realejos ☎ 922 320707

JARDÍN TECINA RESTAURANT (££)
Enjoy lunch with a superb sea view on this wonderful hotel terrace on the south coast of La Gomera.
✉ Lomada de Tecina, Playa de Santiago, La Gomera ☎ 922 145850

LA LANGOSTERA (£–££)
A tempting little fish restaurant where you can enjoy the freshest of simple Canarian cooking.
✉ Paseo Maritimo, Los Abrigos ☎ 922 170302

LAS ROCAS (£££)
The beach club of the Hotel Jardín Tropical provides enjoyable lunches; high-quality seafood.
✉ Calle Gran Bretaña, Costa Adeje ☎ 922 750100

LOS TRONCOS (££)
One of the best restaurants in the Tenerife capital – Canarian cuisine and Basque specialities.
✉ Calle General Goded 17, Santa Cruz ☎ 922 284152

PARADOR DE LA GOMERA (££–£££)
La Gomera's nicely situated parador (1km from San Sebastián) has a stylish dining room and excellent Spanish and international cuisine.
✉ Llano de la Horca, San Sebastián, La Gomera ☎ 922 871100

PARADOR DE LAS CAÑADAS DEL TEIDE (££)
The unpretentious parador restaurant offers good food and is the nearest to Pico del Teide.
✉ Parque Nacional del Teide ☎ 922 386415

RESTAURANTE EL SOMBRERITO (£)
In Chicho and Ana's simple village restaurant high up towards the Cañadas, enjoy wholesome, authentic Tenerife country cooking.
✉ Calle Santa Catalina 15, Vilaflor ☎ 922 709052

TENERIFE
where to...

61

Santa Cruz & Puerto de la Cruz

PRICES

Approximate price of a three-course meal for one, without drinks:

£   = under €18
££ = €18–36
£££ = over €36

SANTA CRUZ

CAFÉ DEL PRÍNCIPE (£–££)

Attractive and authentic place well situated in one of the most appealing squares in Santa Cruz. Sit out with locals and tourists and enjoy a drink, a snack or a complete meal of typical island specialities.
✉ Plaza del Principe de Asturias ☎ 922 278810 🕐 Tue–Sun 9–midnight

EL COTO DE ANTONIO (££)

Rambla del General Franco curves round the city centre. Along here, and northwest of the road, there are several smart eating places catering mainly for business people and well-to-do locals but also tourists. This is a top example, serving good fresh cooking from seasonal ingredients.
✉ Calle General Goded 13 ☎ 922 272105 🕐 Mon–Fri lunch & dinner, Sat dinner. Closed 1–15 Aug

LOS TRONCOS (££)

Among the very best restaurants in the Tenerife capital, in the smart northwest area, and yet surprisingly inexpensive. Noted for Canarian cooking of a high standard, and also for Basque specialities.
✉ Calle General Goded 17 ☎ 922 284152 🕐 Thu–Tue. Closed Sun dinner & mid-Aug to mid-Sep

OLYMPO (£)

This popular bar-restaurant may be touristy, but locals gather here also to enjoy a drink or a meal in a pleasant setting in the heart of town. Good set lunch at a moderate price.
✉ Plaza de la Candelaria ☎ 922 241738 🕐 10AM–midnight

PARQUE MARÍTIMO CÉSAR MANRIQUE (£–£££)

It was part of César Manrique's philosophy that all tourist attractions should offer good eating and drinking facilities on site. The lido on the Santa Cruz waterfront does visitors proud, with a range of eating places from a café to more formal restaurants.
✉ Avenida de la Constitución ☎ 922 202995 🕐 Daily 10–6

PUERTO DE LA CRUZ

CASA DE MIRANDA (££)

This traditional Canarian house near Puerto's harbour square traces its ancestry back to the 1730s. A cheerful *tapas* bar decked with gingham tablecloths, red chilli peppers and hams occupies the ground floor; upstairs its galleried, plant-filled restaurant makes a romantic setting for Canarian and international fare at reasonable prices.
✉ Plaza de Europa ☎ 922 373871 🕐 Lunch, dinner

CASINO TAORO (£££)

Puerto's casino is in Parque Taoro, the park set back from, and above, the bustle of the town. The casino restaurant attracts a dressed-up crowd and caters for them in style, with red-draped tables, formal service, smart atmosphere and a predictable range of classy international dishes. Good views.

✉ Casino, Parque Taoro ☎ 922 380550 ⏰ Dinner

LA PAPAYA (££)

A 200-year-old house in the historic part of town rambles through a series of plant-filled dining rooms and Andalucian-style garden patios. It's a peaceful place, though a caged bird or two may squawk an occasional remark. Seafood and rabbit feature on its menus; the ambience is utterly captivating. Service is friendly.

✉ Calle del Lomo 10 ☎ 922 382811 ⏰ Thu–Tue 12:30–11:30PM

LA PARILLA (£££)

This smart restaurant is located in one of Tenerife's most luxurious hotels, the Botánico, but is open to the public. It offers top of the range international and French-style cooking in an elegant setting. Dress is smart-casual.

✉ Hotel Botánico, Avenida Richard J Yeoward ☎ 922 311400 ⏰ Dinner

LAGO MARTIÁNEZ (£–£££)

Several quality bars and rest-aurants provide a range of snacks, drinks and complete meals in this attractive lake and pool complex (► 30).

✉ Playa Martiánez ☎ 922 383852 ⏰ Daily 10–5, then Andromeda open late in evenings

MAGNOLIA (£££)

Top-class dining, indoors or al fresco, at this award-winning restaurant attracts discerning locals and well-to-do Spanish visitors. Food is a mix of Catalan and international, with an emphasis on fish and seafood. You'll find the restaurant out of town in the La Paz urbanización.

✉ Carretera del Botánico 5, Avenida del Marqués de Villanueva del Prado ☎ 922 385614 ⏰ Dinner

MI VACA Y YO (££)

It looks down to earth and rustic, but this restaurant near the fishing harbour is one of the best in town for exceptional fish and seafood dishes. There are lots of traditional Canarian dishes on the menu, but also a choice of Spanish and international fare.

✉ 3 Calle Cruz Verde ☎ 922 385247 ⏰ Dinner

PALATINO (££)

Excellent seafood in a well-regarded and long-established restaurant. An elegant setting in the old fishing quarter near the Plaza del Charco.

✉ Calle del Lomo 28 ☎ 922 382374 ⏰ Mon–Sat lunch, dinner. Closed Jul

RÉGULO (££)

Popular, atmospheric and attractive with its plants and patio, this is an agreeable example of the many good little fish rest-aurants near the harbour, in the fishermen's quarter near Plaza del Charco.

✉ Calle San Felipe 16 ☎ 922 384506 ⏰ Mon–Sat lunch, dinner. Closed Jul

OPENING TIMES

Although Canarian mealtimes are not as late as those on the mainland, locals often eat lunch at 2PM and dinner at 9PM. *Tapas* are appetisers or between-meal savouries, and should be nibbled with an apéritif during the long hours between lunch and dinner.

63

Around the Island

TAPAS

Tapas are a Spanish institution. Originally a free 'lid' (*tapa*) of ham across a drink, nowadays they consist of small portions of everything from octopus to olives. Locals tend to eat *tapas* before going home for dinner, but several portions can make a filling meal in itself. And you don't have to look at a menu – just point to what you want in the cabinet.

ADEJE

OTELO I (££)

Get a drink or a decent meal at this modest, likeable bar-restaurant brilliantly situated near the entrance to the Barranco del Infierno. Well known to the expatriates and old Tenerife hands, it's especially popular for the island's traditional rabbit dishes, spicy chicken and Canarian specialities. Hearty portions and a pleasant atmosphere.

✉ Calle Los Molinos, Barranco del Infierno ☎ 922 780374
🕐 Wed–Mon 10ᴀᴍ–midnight

BAJAMAR

CAFÉ MELITA (£)

More of a café and cake shop than a restaurant, this German-run place in the little north coast resort specialises in desserts, pastries and rich cakes. Lovely sea views.

✉ Carretera General ☎ 922 540814 🕐 Daily 10–5
🚌 105 (Santa Cruz–Punta Hidalgo) half-hourly

CANDELARIA

EL ARQUETE (££)

There's high-quality creative Canarian cooking at this smarter-than-usual restaurant, something of a find in this part of the island.

✉ Lomo de Aroba 2
☎ 922 500115 🕐 Mon–Sat lunch

EL SAUZAL

CASA DEL VINO (££)

The interesting wine museum and wine-tasting centre in El Sauzal also has a good, lively restaurant, which for some is the main reason to visit. The terrace has sea views.

✉ La Baranda ☎ 922 563886
🕐 Tue–Sat 1–4, 8–midnight, Sun lunch

LA ERMITA (££)

Accomplished seafood and international dishes attract a varied clientele to this quietly set restaurant on the outskirts of town. Local wines are available from the cask. The dining room is smart but relaxing, decorated with plants and ceramics.

✉ Urb. Los Angeles ☎ 922 575380 🕐 Mon–Tue, Thu–Sat lunch, dinner, Sun lunch

GARACHICO

ISLA BAJA (££)

Respected due to its long-standing reputation, this rather pricey restaurant is located on the waterfront facing the Castillo de San Miguel. It specialises in good local fish dishes, though you can also stop by just for a drink, snack or ice-cream.

✉ Calle Esteban de Ponte 5
☎ 922 830008 🕐 Lunch, dinner 🚌 363
(Puerto–Buenavista) hourly

ICOD DE LOS VINOS

CARMEN (££)

Considered the best place to relax, get away from the coach parties, and tuck in to some traditional Spanish cooking before or after peering at the giant Dragon Tree, nearby.

✉ Avenida de Las Canarias 1
☎ 922 810631 🕐 Lunch,

dinner 🚌 354, 363
(Puerto–Icod) both hourly

LA LAGUNA

CASA MAQUILA (££)
La Laguna is not a place
for fine dining, though
there are some good
restaurants out of town.
While sightseeing in the
centre, you should choose a
typical *tapas* bar, and settle
down to local specialities,
properly prepared – at
somewhere like this simple
and agreeable restaurant.
✉ Callejón de Maquila 4
☎ 922 257020 ⏱ Lunch,
dinner

HOYA DEL CAMELLO (££)
It's a short distance out of
town, but this moderately
priced establishment is one
of the La Laguna area's
better restaurants, with a
good range of well-
prepared international,
Spanish and Canarian
favourites.
✉ Carretera General del Norte
128, San Lazaro ☎ 922 262054
⏱ Lunch, dinner. Closed early
May, late Aug, Sun eve

LA OROTAVA

SABOR CANARIO (££)
Set in a fine, late 16th-
century building, this
charming restaurant is
attached to the Museo del
Pueblo Guanche in the
heart of the old town – a
showcase for Canarian
handicrafts and food
products. It serves
authentic local dishes – try
braised rabbit, roast
cheeses or *ropa vieja*
(literally 'old clothes', a
classic Canarian hotpot).

Head for a patio table in
the plant-filled courtyard.
✉ Calle Carrera 17 ☎ 922
323725 ⏱ Mon–Sat lunch,
dinner

LOS ABRIGOS

LA LANGOSTERA (£–££)
Drive past Golf del Sur
developments and down
to the sea. This is just one
of a cluster of tempting
little fish restaurants at
this tiny waterside harbour
along the Costa del
Silencio. Here the fish is
sold by weight: enjoy the
freshest and simplest of
Canarian cooking, with
some good inexpensive
wine.
✉ Paseo Maritimo ☎ 922
170302 ⏱ Lunch, dinner

PERLAS DEL MAR (££)
Of all the fish restaurants
lining the water's edge at
Los Abrigos, this one has
perhaps the best location,
just above the waterline.
Select your fish from the
counter, and specify how
you want it cooked
(steamed, grilled, fried).
Terrace tables make a fine
spot to watch the sun set
over the waves and the
planes landing and taking
off from Reina Sofia
airport.
✉ Paseo Maritimo ☎ 922
170014 ⏱ Lunch, dinner

LOS CRISTIANOS

The resort has scores of
tourist-oriented eating
places, with more of them
reaching a high standard of
service and cuisine than is
the case in neighbouring
Playa de las Américas.

BE POLITE

You'll notice that locals
entering or leaving a
restaurant often address the
room at large with a quiet
greeting of '*Señores, señoras*'.
This is simple politeness.
When speaking to Spaniards, a
formal use of titles is
considered normal, and
makes a good impression
even if your Spanish is not
very good. Address men as
Señor, women as *Señora*, and
young unmarried women as
Señorita.

ETHNIC RESTAURANTS

If you'd rather eat good-quality Italian food than search out Spanish in the heart of the big resorts, life will be easy. The Little Italy chain has nine good restaurants in Playa de las Américas and Los Cristianos – all with Little Italy in their name. If you prefer Chinese, look out for branches of Slow Boat (several in the main southern resorts).

CASA DEL MAR (££)

On a corner of the busy Los Cristianos harbour, this upstairs restaurant offers a good view over the port's activities, and serves a choice of Canarian, Spanish and international favourites.

✉ Esplanade del Muelle ☎ 922 793275 🕓 Tue–Sun lunch, dinner

DON ARMANDO (£)

This Spanish-looking place adds a welcome touch of regional authenticity. Beyond the typically darkish bar (where plenty of Spanish voices can be heard), a light and spacious terrace restaurant hogs grandstand views of the seafront. The all-day menu suggests classic *tapas* like grilled sardines, steamed mussels or potato croquettes, all at moderate prices.

✉ Calle San Telmo ☎ 922 796145 🕓 Daily from lunchtime

LAS GANGARRAS (££)

This attractive restaurant stands in one of the dry ravines behind the resort, amid typically rustic Canarian surroundings. The cooking is classic country style, using some organic produce.

✉ Barranco Oscuro, Buzanada ☎ 922 766423 🕓 Tue–Sat, lunch, dinner

PAPA LUIGI (£–££)

A cosy Italian restaurant in the town centre, cheerfully decorated with terracotta pots and gingham cloths. The menu presents an extensive range of familiar variations on the themes of pasta and pizza, in addition to a selection of fish and meat dishes. Cooking is more than competent, and the service is courteously efficient.

✉ Avenida Suecia 40 ☎ 922 750911 🕓 Lunch, dinner

LOS GIGANTES/ PUERTO DE SANTIAGO

CASA PANCHO (££)

This authentic restaurant comes as a surprise in a popular little sun-and-sea resort area, catering mainly to British people on package holidays and with few signs of any indigenous local life. A genuine Spanish restaurant serving Spanish food to a high standard – there's nowhere else quite as good in the area.

✉ Playa de la Arena ☎ 922 101323 🕓 Jul–May: Tue–Sat lunch, dinner 🚌 473 (Los Gigantes–Las Galletas, south of Los Cristianos)

MIRANDA (££)

Imaginative local and international cuisine in the heart of Los Gigantes. Light, modern décor and a good range of steaks, seafood and Canarian wines.

✉ Calle Flor de Pascua 25 ☎ 922 860207 🕓 Dinner

TAMARA (££)

Grandstand views over the resort and its giant cliffs give this restaurant much of its appeal. The ambience is relaxed and quiet.

✉ Avenida Maritima, Los Gigantes ☎ 922 860011 🕐 Lunch, dinner

LOS NARANJEROS

LOS LIMONEROS (£££)

This rural but very civilised spot off the motorway near La Laguna draws local families for big, well-prepared dinners and weekend feasts of international and local specialities, including rabbit in spicy sauce, and lamb and goat dishes. Service is good.

✉ Carretera General del Norte, Los Naranjeros, 4km east of Tacoronte ☎ 922 636637 🕐 Mon–Sat 12–midnight

MASCA

CHEZ ARLETTE/CASA ENRIQUE (£)

The attractive location on the main road by the church makes this place a local favourite. From its rustic bamboo-shaded terrace decked with simple wooden furnishings stretch magnificent vistas of the gorge below. The menu runs to things like maize cake and grilled lamb, washed down with home-made lemonade or local wines.

✉ La Piedra ☎ 922 863459 🕐 Sun–Fri 11:30AM–6:30PM

PARQUE NACIONAL

EL MESÓN DEL TEIDE (££)

On the Puerto de la Cruz side of the national park, this attractive place pulls in the crowds at lunchtime for wholesome Canarian fare on the steep climb above La Oratava.

✉ Carretera General 821 ☎ 922 354801 🕐 Lunch

RESTAURANTE LAS ESTRELLAS (££)

Out of the crossroads village of Chío, on the southwest side of the national park boundary, this bar-restaurant enjoys stirring views reaching over the coasts.

✉ Chío 🕐 All day 🚌 460 (Icod–Guía de Isora, via Chío) every 2–3 hours

PARADOR LAS CAÑADAS DEL TEIDE (££)

The spectacular *parador* is high in the Park and close to Pico del Teide and all the major volcanic sites. The restaurant is unpretentious but correct, offers good food and is open to the public.

✉ Parque Nacional del Teide ☎ 922 386415 🕐 Lunch, dinner 🚌 343 (Playa de las Américas–Las Cañadas) once daily meets 348 (Puerto–Las Cañadas) once daily

PLAYA DE LAS AMÉRICAS/ COSTA ADEJE

There are literally hundreds of almost identical restaurants along the coast road through the resort. Their basic meals of pasta, pizza, paella, steak or fish and chips, and other international favourites, are displayed in photos on boards outside.

EL MOLINO BLANCO (££)

A white windmill marks

CANARIAN WINE

Tenerife's wines have been drunk in Europe for centuries, traditionally a sweet, rich, heady brew, made from the *malvasia* grape used to make old-fashioned malmsey. Nowadays Tenerife wines can be dry or sweet, red or white. The main wine-growing area is around El Sauzal, just north of Puerto de la Cruz. La Gomera, too, makes drinkable table wine. Make sure you try the sweet dessert wine of Vallehermoso.

'But that which most takes my Muse and me,
Is a pure cup of Canary Wine.'
Ben Jonson, *Epigrammes: Inviting a Friend to Supper* (1616)

GOFIO

Nothing is more Canarian than *gofio*, the versatile staple of the native Guanche diet that is still very much in use. A rough roasted wholemeal flour (usually of maize, but possibly also of barley, wheat, or even chickpeas), it appears in soups, as a sort of polenta, as a paste mixed with vegetables, or as breads, cakes and puddings.

the spot, on the inland side of the resort. Though geared mainly towards foreign tourists, the rustic setting and welcoming atmosphere promise an enjoyable visit. Dining areas spill on to shady flower-filled terraces. Both wine-list and menu are wide-ranging; with unusual items like goat or ostrich.
✉ Avenida de Austria 5, San Eugenio Alto ☎ 922 796282 🕓 Wed–Mon 1PM–1AM

EL PATIO (£££)

Among the very best dining experiences on the south coast. Enjoy a high-quality Canarian and Spanish meal on the terrace of this hotel-restaurant near the Puerto Colón, where Playa de la Américas meets Costa Adeje.
✉ Jardín Tropical Hotel, Calle Gran Bretaña, Urbanización San Eugenio ☎ 922 750100 🕓 Dinner

LA HACIENDA (£££)

One of the elegant restaurants in the luxury hotel complex of the Bahía del Duque. Dress up for a memorable treat.
✉ Gran Hotel Bahía del Duque, Playa del Duque ☎ 922 746900 🕓 Lunch, dinner

MAMMA ROSA (£££)

This very popular restaurant demands a certain smartness from diners to match the good food, fine wine and professional service. Despite the name, the food is not exclusively Italian.

✉ Apartamentos Colón II, Los Moritos ☎ 922 797823 🕓 Lunch, dinner

PORIS DE ABONA

CASABLANCA (££)

Leave the motorway at the Porís exit to track down this spacious pastel-toned restaurant near the seafront. Cuisine includes paella and home-made cheese. Look out for the interesting house wine, Viña Chajaña. Live folk music is an additional draw.
✉ Carretera General ☎ 922 164296 🕓 Tue–Sun lunch, dinner

SAN ISIDRO

EL JABLE (££)

In this untouristy inland village near the motorway, close to the El Médano exit, there's an appealing and popular bar-restaurant serving hearty Canarian cooking.
✉ 9 Calle Bentejui ☎ 922 390698 🕓 Mon–Sat 1–4, 7:30–11. Closed Mon lunch 🚌 111 (Playa de las Américas–Santa Cruz)

SANTA URSULA

LOS CORALES (££)

In the Santa Ursula area, about 10km north of Puerto de la Cruz, several good little restaurants like this specialise in typical Canarian fish stews, and fried eel, as well as a range of more familiar dishes. Local wines accompany the food.
✉ Cuesta de la Villa 30 ☎ 922 302261 🕓 Tue–Sat lunch, dinner

La Gomera

VILAFLOR

EL MIRADOR (£–££)

This restaurant-bar stands just off the road below Mirador de San Roque, by the little Ermitage de San Roque. Enjoy outstanding views and good Canarian cooking.

✉ On C821, Ermita de San Roque ☎ 922 709135
🕐 Lunch 🚌 342 daily from Playa de las Américas; 482 from Los Cristianos; 474 from Granadilla

EL SOMBRERITO (£–££)

The village restaurant of El Sombrerito belongs to Casa Chicho, the family-run inn. In Chicho and Ana's simple, friendly restaurant, you can enjoy authentic Tenerife country recipes. There's a little farm museum and shop attached.

✉ Calle Santa Catalina ☎ 922 709052 🕐 Lunch, dinner
🚌 342 daily from Playa de las Américas; 482 from Los Cristianos; 474 from Granadilla

LA GOMERA

CASA DEL MAR (£–££)

This light, airy bar-restaurant near the seafront serves a large menu of seafood and carefully prepared dishes, attracting local as well as tourist custom. Try the fish stew (*cazuela*). Lighter snacks are also available.

✉ Avenida Fred Olsen 2, San Sebastián ☎ 922 871219
🕐 Mon–Sat lunch, dinner

HOTEL JARDÍN TECINA RESTAURANT (££)

The terrace of this excellent hotel on La Gomera's south coast offers international dining and a wonderful view of the sea.

✉ Lomada de Tecina, Playa de Santiago ☎ 922 145850
🕐 Lunch, dinner

LAS ROSAS (££)

Not just a place to eat, this pretty roadside restaurant is an essential stopover on a tour of La Gomera. Its superb valley-edge location and views and, most of all, its fascinating demonstrations of *el silbo* (➤ 49), the island's unique whistling language, attract coach parties every day. However, the Canarian specialities are delightful too.

✉ Las Rosas ☎ 922 800916
🕐 Lunch

EL SILBO (£)

This modest bar-restaurant stands on the main road just north of the village. Its flower-decked terrace is a charming spot to enjoy an inexpensive drink or meal with a view.

✉ Hermigua ☎ 922 880304
🕐 Tue–Sun lunch, dinner

PARADOR DE SAN SEBASTIÁN DE LA GOMERA (££–£££)

This parador (➤ 75) has the best food on the island; Spanish and international cuisine.

✉ Llano de la Horca 1 ☎ 922 871100 🕐 Lunch, dinner

MOJO

One of the most genuinely Canarian words on the menu is *mojo*. Meat, fish and vegetables may all be served *con mojo*, with mojo, the piquant sauce that comes in different versions, more or less spicy according to what it accompanies. The two main types are *mojo verde*, green mojo, its parsley and coriander recipe giving a cool, sharp flavour, and *mojo rojo*, the spicier, red sauce made with chillis and peppers. Grilled goat's cheese, too, is served *con mojo*.

69

Santa Cruz & Puerto de la Cruz

PRICES

For a double room in mid-season expect to pay:

£   = under €72
££   = €72–120
£££ = over €120

ON THE CARDS

Credit cards are widely accepted in both large and small shops in Santa Cruz, Puerto de la Cruz and the Playa de las Américas area. In other towns, and all over La Gomera, expect to be told only cash is acceptable.

SANTA CRUZ

ATLÁNTICO (£)

This modest, pleasant, Spanish-oriented hotel, locally defined as a two-star, is adequately equipped, reasonably priced, and well placed in the main shopping street at the heart of the city.
✉ Calle Castillo 12 ☎ 922 246375; fax 922 246378

CONTEMPORANÉO (£)

A modern three-star hotel almost free of English or German voices. Rooms are pleasantly furnished and equipped, and there's a restaurant and snack bar.
✉ Rambla General Franco 116 ☎ 922 271571; fax 922 271223

MENCEY (£££)

Mencey means a Guanche chieftain, and this elegant hotel is the chief among Tenerife's traditional five-star accommodation. In sumptuous colonial style with lavish marble, fine woodwork and artworks on display, the hotel offers every possible amenity: the location is peaceful, away from the city centre on the north side of the Ramblas.
✉ Avenida Doctor José Naveiras 38 ☎ 922 276700; fax 922 280017

PELINOR (£)

This is a good example of a smaller, less expensive hotel, located in the heart of the city close to Plaza de España and aimed chiefly at Spanish visitors. The neat and comfortable rooms have TVs, and there's a bar on site.
✉ Calle Béthencourt Alphonso 8 ☎ 922 246875; fax 922 280520

PLAZA (££)

Located in an agreeable square in the centre of the city, close to shops, restaurants and entertainment, this comfortable, reasonably priced hotel makes a good base in the city.
✉ Plaza de la Candelaria 10 ☎ 922 272453; fax 922 275160

TABURIENTE (££)

An aura of old-world grandeur clings to this long-established, classically furnished hotel. Many of its rooms have attractive views over Parque García Sanabria and the main sights lie within walking distance.
✉ Avenida Doctor José Naveiras 24A ☎ 922 276000; fax 922 270562

PUERTO DE LA CRUZ

BOTÁNICO (£££)

An exceptional hotel of relaxed elegance, offering the height of luxury and modern facilities. On the northeast side of town, it's quite a long way from the centre and from the sea. Five stars, and a member of the Leading Hotels of the World group.
✉ Avenida Richard Yeoward, Urbanización Botánico 1 ☎ 922 381400; fax 922 381504

MARQUESA (££)

The waterfront street of the original Puerto saw the creation of this hotel in 1712, long before the advent of tourism. It's been a hotel ever since, still relatively simple, but much modernised, with a swimming pool and restaurant. It's thoroughly charming, and keeps much of its colonial-era atmosphere.

✉ Calle Quintana 11 ☎ 922 383151; fax 922 386950

MONOPOL (££)

One of the town's earliest hotels, by the waterfront in the historic heart of town. Though much modernised, including a swimming pool, it retains a pleasing colonial feel, with cane furnishings and greenery on a charming patio.

✉ Calle Quintana 15 ☎ 922 384611; fax 922 370310

SAN FELIPE (£££)

One of Puerto's best hotels, long established but thoroughly modernised. The high-rise San Felipe is owned by the prestigious Melia group. A huge range of facilities and services is on offer, with children's activities, nightly entertainment, and well-equipped rooms.

✉ Avenida de Colón 22 ☎ 922 383311; fax 922 373718

SAN TELMO (£)

Spectacular views of the rocky coast. Though it has nearly a hundred bedrooms, this family-managed hotel still has an intimate, personal feel. The decor combines nautical themes with floral chintz and the restaurant is cosy with wood panelling and fretwork screens. The pool on the rooftop sun terrace is undersized, but it's only a short stroll to the famous Lago. The simple

bedrooms are light and spacious with good bathrooms.

✉ Paseo San Telmo 18 ☎ 922 385853; fax 922 385991

SEMIRAMIS (£££)

This ambitious five-star hotel, up the coast from Playa Martiánez, is some distance from the centre of town but has fine sea views from some rooms and offers every modern comfort and facility.

✉ Leopoldo Cólogan Zulueta 12 ☎ 922 373200; fax 922 373193

TIGAIGA (£££)

In the gorgeous garden setting of the Taoro Park area, above the town, this conventional tourist hotel has won awards for its environmental management. One of its claims is that the hotel has more palm trees than beds. Unremarkable but comfortable rooms have partial sea views and face either the Taoro Park or Pico del Teide. The pool area has a view over Puerto, and there's a separate terrace for topless sunbathing.

✉ 28 Parque Taoro ☎ 922 383500; fax 922 384055

TIMESHARE DREAMS

Tenerife is timeshare land, where touts pester, lure and tempt the unwary into signing away their savings in exchange for a-week-a-year at a resort apartment block. Lavish inducements are given, not just to sign, but even to see the property. Timeshare is not a bad idea in principle – you don't have to use your annual week or two weeks; you can rent them out, or swap them for a fortnight in Florida or Florence. Don't agree to pay anything without legal advice, and be sure you are informed about Spanish property law and taxes.

Where to Stay

71

Around the Island

PACKAGE DEAL

Playa de las Américas, Costa Adeje and Los Cristianos run into each other along the coast, effectively creating a single resort area – often known collectively as Playa de las Américas. Only Los Cristianos had any existence before the tourism boom took off in the late 1960s. Today the three areas consist almost entirely of scores of hotels, holiday apartments and 'aparthotels'. Almost all visitors arrive on an inclusive package with pre-booked accommodation – and that is the simplest and cheapest way to come to this part of Tenerife. However, the hotels listed here can usually be booked independently, as well as through tour operators.

GOLF COAST

Several golf links are located around Playa de las Américas. Just east of the resort, the quiet new villa and hotel development of Golf del Sur, though in a rather bleak location close to the former fishing village of Los Abrigos, has the advantage of being only 5km from Reina Sofía airport and near to high-quality golf links.

COSTA ADEJE

GRAN HOTEL ANTHELIA PARK (£££)

This grandiose modern resort complex consists of six small hotel blocks catering to slightly different markets. For example, one is for families, one is quiet, one consists only of luxury suites and so on. All the rooms have a sea view, and the whole place is equipped with a wealth of amenities and services. There are five pools, three restaurants, several bars, a kindergarten and a nightclub, as well as more unusual features, such as a library. Playa del Duque is a few minutes walk away.
✉ Calle de Londres, Playa del Duque ☎ 922 713335; fax 922 719081

COLÓN GUANAHANI (£££)

An attractive low-rise building in neo-classical style, with marble columns and arches, this hotel is in the western part of Costa Adeje. Green tile pathways wander among shrubs and palm trees, and the heated seawater pool is pleasantly surrounded by trees. There's a good restaurant, plenty of facilities, entertainment and a children's club. Playa de Fañabé is about 150m away.
✉ Calle Bruselas, Playa de la Fañabé ☎ 922 712046; fax 922 712121

GRAN HOTEL BAHÍA DEL DUQUE (£££)

One of Tenerife's most extravagant hotels occupies a large secluded plot north of Playa de Fañabe. This elaborate five-star complex consists of some 20 separate, individually designed buildings in Mediterranean and Canarian styles. The reception lobby is an eyecatching space of aviaries, fountains, exotic flowers and murals, and within the beautifully kept grounds the turretted accommodation blocks and multiple restaurants promise a hedonistic stay. Guests enjoy direct access to an immaculate beach boasting an adventurous selection of watersports.
✉ Calle Alcalde Walter Paetzmann s/n ☎ 922 766933; fax 922 746925

JARDÍN TROPICAL (£££)

Located at the Puerto Colón end of the Playa de Troya, where Playa de las Américas meets up-market Costa Adeje, the award-winning Jardín Tropical is a superb resort hotel. Its imaginative white Moorish appearance, beautiful pool area, lush colourful vegetation and seafront location add up to a wonderful, luxurious place to stay on the south coast. There are five restaurants within the hotel.
✉ Calle Gran Bretaña ☎ 922 746000; fax 746060

JARDINES DE NIVARIA (£££)

Situated over in the quieter, western end of the resort, near Playa del Duque and Playa de

Fañabé, the designers of this hotel have tried to incorporate some local themes into its architectural design. Tiles and polished wood feature in the rooms. There is an attractive pool area with seawater pools (one heated in winter).
✉ Calle Paris ☎ 922 713333; fax 922 713340

GARACHICO

SAN ROQUE (£££)
One of the most unusual and delightful hotels on the island, this historic building stands in the middle of the waterfront. The place has an exquisite low-key elegance. Armchairs and potted plants are dotted about, and there's a lovely arcaded and balconied courtyard at the middle of the building. There are 20 well-equipped rooms.
✉ Calle Esteban de Ponte 32 ☎ 922 133435; fax 922 133406

GOLF DEL SUR

LAS ADELFAS (££)
Near the airport and Los Abrigos village, the aparthotel borders the PGA-approved 27-hole Golf del Sur course. Accommodation is in a cluster of two-storey blocks designed to look like Spanish villas. They have kitchens, simple furnishings and satellite TV, and enclosed pools, a restaurant and a bar.
✉ Urbanización Golf del Sur (take San Miguel de Abona turn off highway) ☎ 922 738616; fax 738444

TENERIFE GOLF (££)
The hotel stands at the seafront of this coastal development near the airport, with air-conditioned rooms, all with balcony and cable TV. There's a buffet restaurant, a seawater pool (heated in winter), tennis court and entertainment.
✉ Urbanización Golf del Sur (take San Miguel de Abona turn off highway) ☎ 922 738566; fax 922 738889

LA LAGUNA

NIVARIA (£)
In a town with few hotels suitable for holiday-makers, the reasonably equipped three-star Aparthotel Nivaria is an acceptable possibility. It has no restaurant, but is well placed in the old centre of town close to all amenities.
✉ 11 Plaza del Adelantado ☎ 922 264298

LOS CRISTIANOS

ESTEFANIA (£££)
Behind the arid Arona coastline, the road corkscrews steeply upwards into the hills. This elegant retreat rests in a sloping, flower-filled site with extensive views down to the ocean. The shady pool terrace is set with white wicker, the gardens artfully landscaped with statuary and fountains. Bedrooms are cool and classy in black Italianate furnishings.
✉ Urb. Las Aguilas del Teide, Chayofa ☎ 922 729322; fax 922 751593

EL CALABAZO

Water is scarce on the Canaries. To deal with the problem, Tenerife farmers used a simple method of scooping water from canals, irrigation ditches or waterways into a tank and taking it to their crops. The men who scooped the water became very skilled, and were called *calabaceros*. The practice died out in the 1970s, but *calabazo* contests have become common at fiestas, with contestants seeing how quickly they can transfer water with a scoop. The scoops today are usually metal bowls, but the traditional tool was, of course, a *calabazo* (pumpkin).

CLASS ACT

Playa de las Américas, the ultimate mass-market resort, has good family accommodation and entertainment but also has its share of bierkellers, lager louts and garish late-night entertainment. Los Cristianos, east of Playa de las Américas, has always been considered a little more select. In contrast to these two, the newer development of Costa Adeje, north of Playa de las Américas, aims to be a little classier, with higher prices, more style, some beautiful landscaping and several modern neoclassical-style hotels.

STRIP OFF

Topless sunbathing is acceptable at all Tenerife beaches, pools and lidos, especially at the main resorts. Naturism, or stripping off completely, is never acceptable on resort beaches, but common on any secluded stretch of coast, or beaches outside resorts. Certain hotels at Puerto de la Cruz and Playa de las Américas have secluded separate sunbathing terraces specifically for nude sunbathing.

OASIS MOREQUE (£££)

Inside, this older-style block in the resort centre is rather nicer than its exterior suggests, tastefully decorated in bright, contemporary fabrics and wicker chairs, with a delightful conservatory-style restaurant. Small and friendly, it's constantly popular with families. The rear grounds are pleasing too, with plenty of mature greenery, though not large.
✉ Avenida Penetración s/n
☎ 922 790366; fax 922 792260

LOS GIGANTES

TAMAIMO TROPICAL (££)

This large but secluded complex stands on a quiet site near the Los Gigantes marina and the fine beach of Playa de la Arena. The well-maintained apartment buildings, designed with Canarian-style balconies, shutters and pantiles, are set around two spacious pool terraces with natural shade. Individual units are well-equipped and tastefully decorated with stylish lamps, rugs and tiles. There's a conservatory restaurant, though there are plenty of eating places nearby.
✉ Calle Hondura, Puerto de Santiago ☎ 922 860638; fax 922 860761

PARQUE NACIONAL

PARADOR DE LAS CAÑADAS DEL TEIDE (£££)

Tenerife's only *parador* occupies a stunning location near the foot of Pico del Teide, and makes an exceptional touring and walking base. Recently refurbished and upgraded, the hotel merges unobtrusively into the surrounding sandy plains, and picture windows overlook a startling array of weirdly eroded rocks. Inside, the hotel is comfortably cheerful, with exposed stonework and open fires to ward off the chill of the altitude. Bedrooms are spacious and well equipped.
✉ Parque Nacional del Teide
☎ 922 386415; fax 922 382352

PLAYA DE LAS AMÉRICAS

BITÁCORA (££)

One of the big popular holiday hotels, the Bitácora has a spacious pool and lawn, plenty of attractions and facilities for families, and generous buffets.
✉ Avenida Antonio Domínguez Alfonso 1 ☎ 922 791540; fax 922 796677

LAS DALIAS (££)

The huge and popular Las Dalias (800 beds) offers a poolside terrace, paella at the afternoon barbecue and a nightly disco. Nearby Los Hibiscos, Bougainville Playa and Torviscas Playa hotels are similar – all are in the Sungarden group, and all use the same booking numbers.
✉ Calle Gran Bretaña ☎ 922 792712; fax 922 797675

La Gomera

There are only a limited number of hotels and pensiones on the island, and most of the accomodation involves staying in homes or private apartments. *Casas rurales* are former farmhouses converted to rental properties (☎ 922 595019).

IBO ALFARO (£)

This delightful rural hostelry is on a quiet track above a valley village. The 19th-century building has been renovated in traditional Canarian style using natural stone and timber. Breakfast is served on a terrace in fine weather. Bedrooms have tasteful plain walls, wooden shutters and tiled bathrooms.

✉ Hermigua ☎ 922 880168; fax 922 881019

JARDÍN TECINA (£££)

This top-class hotel clings to a clifftop, with magnificent gardens of native plantlife (everything is labelled, as in a botanical park). It has a beautiful pool, and stirring views over the strait to Tenerife, with Pico del Teide rising in the distance. The 'rooms' are in delightful cottages in the grounds.

✉ Lomada de Tecina, Playa de Santiago ☎ 922 145850; fax 922 145851

PARADOR DE SAN SEBASTIÁN DE LA GOMERA (£££)

La Gomera's attractive *parador* stands high above the port up a steeply winding road. The building is a convincing copy of an early colonial mansion. Furnishings are typically Castilian (carved chests and terracotta tiles). Canarian specialities like parrot fish with *mojo* and flambéed bananas feature on the menu. The subtropical clifftop gardens to the rear command huge views over the town and the local coast, with Pico del Teide on the horizon.

✉ Llano de la Horca 1, San Sebastián ☎ 922 871100; fax 922 871116

JARDÍN DEL CONDE (££)

Low-rise apartments surround a large pool terrace on the landward side of Valle Gran Rey's promenade. This attractive complex is brightly landscaped with lots of greenery and flowering plants. A useful mini-market and bar is located near the entrance, and there are plenty of eating places nearby.

✉ Avenida Marítima, Valle Gran Rey ☎ 922 806008; fax 922 805385

HOTEL DE TRIANA (£)

The plain exterior of this modest house in a residential street belies its contemporary décor of cool, soothing colours, plain walls and exposed stonework. Bedrooms feature mosaic-tiled bathrooms, and some have kitchenettes. A small restaurant provides home-cooked cuisine.

✉ Calle Triana, Vallehermoso ☎ 922 800528; fax 922 800128

SPEAK THE LANGUAGE?

The official language of the Canaries is Castilian Spanish, but the local dialect has many distinguishing features. Most striking is the complete absence of the normal Spanish 'th' sound (as in 'think'), which is usually written as 'ce'. In the Canaries, the letters 'ce' are pronounced as 's'. Another characteristic is the frequent use of Portuguese words, the result of the close relations between the Canaries and Latin America.

EL SILBO

Of all the distinctive elements in Canarian culture, few are more astonishing than the 'whistling language' of La Gomera. In response to similar conditions that gave rise to yodelling in Switzerland – needing to communicate across steep terrain and dense forests – the Gomerans developed a whole vocabulary, syntax and grammar of whistles. Another quality of *el silbo* is its volume: skilled *silbadores* can whistle a detailed message to another person several kilometres away.

Handicrafts & Souvenirs

UNUSUAL SOUVENIRS

Choose from banana-shaped bottles of sugary *cobana* (banana liqueur), dolls in national costume, items made from palm leaves, or banana-leaf baskets. Also woodcarving, leatherware, prettily packaged sweets and biscuits or bottles of spicy *mojo* sauce, local wines, cigars or plant souvenirs like baby dragon tress, and bird-of-paradise flowers are all worth looking out for.

DUTY & TAX

Although the Canary Islands are a duty-free area, it doesn't follow that all goods are free of tax. Prices are bumped up by the local IGIC tax, which puts 5 per cent on the value of goods and is sometimes not included in window-display prices.

EMBROIDERY, LACE & THREADWORK

The Canaries are known for exquisite embroidery (*bordados*) and fine threadwork (*calados*) and decorative lacework, especially doilies (*rosetas*). Exceptional patience and skill are required of the local women who do the work. However, you should beware of street sellers and market traders offering inferior low-priced imported factory-made embroidery.

POTTERY

Canarian potters traditionally didn't use the potter's wheel, and still today on Tenerife and La Gomera highly skilled local potters working entirely by hand produce distinctive household objects and decorative items. Look out in the craft shops for their *gánigos* – household pots made without a potter's wheel – and necklaces and other jewellery decorated with Guanche symbols.

WICKERWORK

Local handmade Tenerife basketwork is distinctive and pretty, and makes a good choice for souvenirs. Skilled wickerwork craftsmen and women can be seen working in the many craft fairs.

SHOPS

A range of all these locally made items can be found at the following craft stores. It may be worth shopping around, as the stock varies from place to place. Shop hours are generally Mon–Sat 9–1, 4–8.

COSTA ADEJE

CASA DE LOS BALCONES
A wide range of inexpensive crafts.
✉ Gran Hotel Bahía del Duque Fañabe

LA LAGUNA

CASA DE LOS CALADOS
✉ Calle Núñez de la Peña 9

LA OROTAVA

CASA DE LOS BALCONES
This beautifully restored 17th-century mansion (➤ 25) contains a craft shop, where local people can often be seen at work. As well as inexpensive souvenirs, a wide range of high-quality items, such as Spanish and Canarian lace and linen and traditional Canarian embroideries, are on sale. Some are made on the premises, as the Casa de los Balcones also serves as a school of embroidery.
✉ 3 Calle San Francisco

CASA TORREHERMOSA
This is run by the state-

run crafts organisation, Empresa Insular de Artesanía del Cabildo de Tenerife, and specialises in genuine local work. There is a craft museum attached.
✉ Calle Tomás Zerolo 27, La Orotava ☎ 922 334013

CASA DEL TURISTA
Located opposite La Orotava's famous Casa de los Balcones (➤ above), this craft and souvenir shop has the same owners and stocks similar products.
✉ Calle San Francisco 4, La Orotava

PUERTO DE LA CRUZ

ARTESANÍA DEL LINO
✉ Calle Santo Domingo

CASA DE LOS BALCONES
✉ Paseo de San Telmo 22

CASA IRIARTE
The disorganised store in this historic building has a fine selection of hand-worked table linen.
✉ Calle San Juan 17

SANTA CRUZ

ARTE TENERIFE
✉ Plaza de España

ARTESANÍA CELSA
✉ Calle Castillo 8

CASA DE LOS BALCONES
✉ Edificio Olympo, Plaza de la Candelaria

MERCADO DE ARTESANÍA ESPAÑOLA
✉ Plaza de la Candelaria 8

VILAFLOR

MERCADO DE ARTESANÍA ESPAÑOLA
An interesting stop on the way into the Teide National Park.
✉ Carretera General 🕒 All year

LA GOMERA

ARTESANÍA LOS TELARES
See weaving and other local crafts in production before you buy. There is a similar *artenesía* at Agulo, the next village about 3km away.
✉ Hermigua 🕒 Mon–Sat

MARKET
Gomeran craftwork and local products at the morning market.
✉ Avenida de Colón, San Sebastián

SUMMER FAIRS
Have fun while looking for souvenirs at these summer fairs, or *ferias artesanía*.

Los Realejos	May, Jun
Güimar	Jun
La Orotava	Jun
El Sauzal	Jun/Jul
La Laguna	Jul
Santiago del Teide	Jul
Arona/Los Cristianos	Jul/Aug
Fasnia	Aug
El Rosario	Aug
Garachico	Aug
La Victoria de Acentejo	Aug
Buenavista del Norte	Aug
La Matanza	Aug
Vilaflor	Aug/Sep
San Juan de la Rambla	Sep
San Miguel de Abona	Sep
Guía de Isora	Sep
Tacoronte	Sep
El Tanque	Oct

GOMERAN POTS
La Gomera continues traditional methods of making handmade pots without a potter's wheel. One of the villages best known for this is tiny El Cercado, high on a narrow, winding road in the west of the island. Many of its simple cottages are pottery workshops, where the pots are made from the island's striking dark red clay.

A TASTE OF HONEY
One of the strangest specialities in the Canaries is the palm-tree 'honey' of La Gomera. Not real honey, *miel de palma* is made like maple syrup. The *guarapo*, or sap, of the date palm is tapped, then boiled. The result is a dark syrup, rich, tasty and sweet. Buy it where you see signs at smallholdings around the island, or in the market at San Sebastián.

Bargains & Markets

HYPERMARKET SHOPPING

Self-caterers will sometimes prefer to go to a supermarket to make shopping easy. The Continente *centro comercial* not only has a huge hypermarket with a vast range of goods at reasonable prices, but there are also 100 other shops on the site. The Continente is 5km south of Santa Cruz, by Junction 4 (Santa Maria del Mar exit) of the Autopista del Sur (⊙ Mon–Sat 10–10).

OUT OF AFRICA

Colourfully dressed West Africans hawking on the beaches, in the streets and selling in the markets and fairs of Tenerife add an exotic note. These traders are often Senegalese, make the boat trip specifically to sell in European markets and stay for several months. Usually they all sell very similar goods: leatherwork, carved toys, African drums, beads and, at higher prices, often illegally exported tribal artefacts, including ceremonial masks. What not to buy: ivory – many African traders offer ivory items, but these are illegal throughout the EU, with heavy fines and confiscation of the goods if found by customs officers.

BARGAINS

As a duty-free region, the Canary Islands sell perfumes, cameras, binoculars and other optical goods, CD players and electronic items at lower prices than at home. In the big towns and main resorts, several Asian-run 'Bazaars' are the usual outlet for these goods. Marked prices are generally open to a bit of haggling, though some shops make a point of not negotiating – a bonus for Europeans who dread haggling! Prices are similar to those in airports and other duty-free outlets. Before buying, it helps to know what the price is at home, and whether the guarantee will be valid. The main outlets are: Calle de Castillo, Santa Cruz; Playa de las Américas; Puerto de la Cruz.

MARKETS & HAWKERS

Genuine markets, like the Mercado Nuestra Señora de África (➤ 33), are the place to find fresh fruit and vegetables, kitchenware, fabrics and household items. Most other Tenerife markets attract European hippy 'artists' and African traders, selling a repetitive range of kitsch, beads and home-made jewellery, and leather goods. Some of them occasionally offer original or interesting items. They are often joined by Spanish stallholders offering either bargain clothes, beachwears, or lace, crochet and embroidery, especially tablecloths, placemats, napkins, bedlinen and handkerchiefs. These are not always offered at low prices, but they represent good value for such high-quality handmade work. You may also find glazed pottery and crockery, attractively hand-painted. When not at the markets, the hippies and African traders often hawk their goods in streets and on the beaches.

MAIN MARKETS

LOS ABRIGOS
Night market.
⊙ Tue 6–10

LOS CRISTIANOS
✉ Next to Hotel Gran Arona
⊙ Sun 9–2

PLAYA DE LAS AMÉRICAS
✉ Torviscas, Playa de las Américas ⊙ Thu, Sat 9–2

PUERTO DE LA CRUZ
Mercado Municipal San Felipe.
✉ Avenida de Blas Pérez Gonzáles ⊙ Mon–Sat AM

SANTA CRUZ
Mercado Nuestra Señora de África (➤ 33).
✉ Calle de San Sebastián ⊙ Mon–Sat 8–1

Rastro (flea market).
✉ Near the *mercado*, Calle José Manuel Guimerá ⊙ Sun 10–2

SAN SEBASTIÁN, LA GOMERA
✉ Avenida de Colón
⊙ Mon–Sat AM

TACORONTE
Farmers' market.
⊙ Sat PM, Sun AM

Excursions

ARTS & DRAMA

Tenerife has several art galleries, museums, concert halls and theatres. Most of the island's culture is located in the north.

LA LAGUNA

The town of La Laguna, little frequented by tourists, is Tenerife's centre of contemporary culture.

TEATRO LEAL

Hosts annual festivals of jazz, folk music and international theatre.
☒ Calle Obispo Rey Redondo

SANTA CRUZ

AUDITORIO

A state-of-the-art concert hall opened in 2002.
☒ Near the Parque Marítimo César Manrique

TEATRO GUIMERÁ

Plays (Spanish-language only), opera and concerts – and home of the first-class Symphony Orchestra of Tenerife, which gives performances all year.
☒ Plaza Isla de la Madora
☎ 922 606265

BOAT EXCURSIONS

Many tour operators and local travel firms organise boat excursions from Los Cristianos, Playa de las Américas, Costa Adeje and Costa del Silencio. Day trips to La Gomera are especially popular and enjoyable. Other boat trips have no goal except fun, such as the many *sangréa* excursions and pirate adventures, which include lunch and usually a swimming stop.

YELLOW SUBMARINE

A trip in a semi-submersible to explore the seas around southern Tenerife (► 57).
☒ South Pier, Puerto Colón, Playa de las Américas ☎ 922 715080 ⓒ Hourly trips 10–4 🚌 Free shuttle bus from southern resorts and Aquapark

TOURS

See panel, Coach Tours, for suggestions.

WHALEWATCHING

About 200 pilot whales live in Canary Island waters, usually on the south side of the archipelago. An easy place to spot whales is between Los Cristianos and Los Gigantes; dolphins can also be found. Boat trips to see them are among the highlights for visitors.

NOSTRAMO

Successful and popular boat excursions in a beautiful Spanish schooner built in 1918. As well as seeing dolphins and whales, the leisurely outing is unforgettable for the lunch below the Los Gigantes cliffs and a pause in Masca Bay for a chance to swim.
☒ Playa San Juan, Playa de las Américas ☎ 922 750085 (Playa de las Américas), 922 385116 (Puerto de la Cruz) ⓒ Departs daily 10AM 🚌 Free bus from southern resorts

TROPICAL DELFIN

Modern excursion boat with underwater windows to view the sealife.
☒ South Pier, Puerto Colón, Playa de las Américas ☎ 922 75 0149 ⓒ Daily 10:30, 1:30

COACH TOURS

Organised bus or coach tours are a popular way of exploring the landscapes of Tenerife The most rewarding tours include a trip to Pico del Teide; across the Macizo de Teno to Masca; and a day out in Santa Cruz. If you are staying in Playa de las Américas, a day trip to Puerto de la Cruz, including Loro Parque and Bananera El Guanche, is highly enjoyable. Another worthwhile tour is the day out on La Gomera. These tours are available from hotel reception desks and through tour operators' reps at the resorts.

WHALEWATCHING TIPS

• Only travel with boat firms licensed to run excursions (like the two included on this page).
• Boats should not get too close to whales.
• Engines should be turned off when near whales.
• Don't change direction frequently – this irritates the whales.
• Don't throw anything at whales (and do not throw litter into the sea).
• Don't swim with whales – remember, they are wild animals.

Sport

PEACEFUL ISLAND

In contrast to the lively scene on its larger neighbour, little La Gomera has almost no organised sport, entertainment or nightlife. Some of the hotels do put on low-key shows, and there are small discos. Tourists, like locals, must rely on fiestas for music, folklore and fun.

GOLF

Many visitors come to Tenerife purely in order to play golf on the excellent golf courses, four of which are in the area between Playa de las Américas and the airport. If you are playing and staying in the south, visit the northern golf course at least once – for the amazing contrast of lush greenery. Each of the golf courses has formed partnerships with nearby hotels, whose resident guests enjoy reduced green fees (enquire at the clubs for details).

NORTH

REAL CLUB DE GOLF TENERIFE

An 18-hole course founded in 1932 by British expatriates.
✉ El Peñon, Tacoronte (2km from Los Rodeos airport, 14km from Santa Cruz) ☎ 922 636607;
www.realgolfdetenerife.com

SOUTH

AMARILLA GOLF

An 18-hole course, bordered by coastal cliffs.
✉ Urbanización Amarilla Golf, San Miguel de Abona ☎ 922 730319

CENTRO DE GOLF LOS PALOS

A nine-hole course (par 27) near Playa de las Américas. Small but challenging.
✉ Carretera Guaza–Las Galletas km 7, Arona ☎ 922 169080

COSTA ADEJE GOLF

This fine 27-hole course is located 5km from Playa de las Américas, with views of La Gomera.
✉ Finca de los Olivos, Adeje ☎ 922 710000

GOLF DEL SUR

This 27-hole course has hosted several international events.
✉ Urbanización Golf del Sur, San Miguel de Abona ☎ 922 738170

GOLF LAS AMÉRICAS

An 18-hole course (par 72) just outside Playa de las Américas and Los Cristianos.
✉ Exit 28 from Autopista del Sur ☎ 922 752005

WATER SPORTS

Scuba and offshore diving is popular all around the islands. Several centres offer a good standard and are staffed by qualified instructors. Diving courses should meet PADI standards and also check insurance cover.

BARLOVENTO

Canoeing, sailing, water-skiing, windsurfing and boat hire.
✉ Parque Marítimo César Manrique, Santa Cruz ☎ 922 223840

CENTRO DE BUCEO ATLANTIK

✉ Hotel Maritim, Calle El Burgado 1, Puerto de la Cruz ☎ 922 362801

CENTRO INSULAR DE DEPORTES MARINOS (CIDEMAT)

Canoeing, diving, sailing, water-skiing and windsurfing.
✉ Carretera Santa Cruz–San Andrés ☎ 922 240945

CLUB NAUTICO
✉ Avenida de Anaga, Santa Cruz ☎ 922 240945

NAUTIOCIO
Jet skiing, parascending, sailing, water-skiing and banana boats.
✉ Puerto Colón, Costa Adeje ☎ 922 714034

SUNWIND
Near-constant trade winds and warm unpolluted waters ensure ideal conditions for windsurfing and surfing around the island's south coast. One of the best locations is El Médano beach, on the south coast. Waters on the north coast are too rough for safe surfing.
✉ Avenida Islas Canarias, El Médano ☎ 922 176174

WALKING, CLIMBING & CYCLING
Graded footpaths marked and maintained by ICONA, the Spanish conservation agency, criss-cross the island. The agency issues a number of maps (available in tourist offices and park visitor centres) showing marked walks. These include a pack of 22 footpath maps, with descriptions in English about each area and the landmarks, flora and fauna. Discovery Walking Guides and Sunflower Guides (available in the UK) are useful for walkers. See the panel, right.

ADEN TENERIFE MULTIAVENTURA
This highly proficient multi-adventure sports centre organises cycling tours, mountain cycling, horse riding, walking excursions and climbing.
✉ Calle Castillo (Oficina 307) 41, Santa Cruz ☎ 922 246261

GAIATOURS
A well-known trekking operator offering a regular weekly programme of guided walks in interesting parts of Tenerife.
☎ 922 355272

GREGORIO
An established escorted walks specialist, offering over 50 routes for all ages and fitness levels.
✉ Hotel Tigaiga, Parque Taoro 28, Puerto de la Cruz ☎ 922 383500

WRESTLING
One of the traditional island sports, called *la lucha* or *lucha canaria*, is a curious form of wrestling. With its own weekly TV show, and frequent matches, Canarian Wrestling has become very popular in recent years. Two teams compete by pitting one man against another, in turns, until there is a clear victory. The men, wearing a particular style of shorts and shirt, try to throw each other to the ground by gripping each other's clothing. Tourists are welcome to watch matches: ask at hotels or tourist office for match details and venues. Demonstrations are given at the Hotel Tigaiga.
✉ Parque Taoro 28, Puerto de la Cruz ☎ 922 383500
🕐 Sun 11AM

WALKING ADVICE
ICONA, the outdoor activities and conservation agency, give the following advice to walkers in Tenerife:
• Take a hat and sunglasses
• Take water to drink
• Don't pick any plants
• Let someone know about your walk
• Never walk without a map (available from Puerto de la Cruz and Santa Cruz tourist offices, and Teide National Park Visitor Centre; ☎ 922 290129)

Nightlife

A NIGHT IN

Most tourist hotels, especially
the larger places, offer music,
shows and entertainment on
the premises every evening.
Some can be quite
spectacular, with a cabaret-
style floorshow and dancers.
Flamenco and colourful
folklore shows are common.
Several hotels also host loud,
atmospheric discos for the
younger crowd.

CHAMPION COCKTAIL

Puerto's Casino Taoro won the
1988 Spanish National Cocktail
Contest for its house drink,
called Cocktail Taoro. It's a
sizzling, hilarious, extravagant
and drinkable mix of
champagne, calvados and
banana liqueur with lemon
and caviar.

CASINOS

CASINO PLAYA DE LAS AMÉRICAS
Place your bets at the
Hotel Gran Tinerfe.
✉ Avenida Rafael Puig Llurina,
Playa de las Américas ☎ 922
793758 🕐 From 7PM

CASINO SANTA CRUZ
Dress up for an evening of
roulette, blackjack and
poker at Tenerife's
poshest hotel.
✉ Hotel Mencey, Avenida Doctor
José Naveiras 38, Santa Cruz
☎ 922 276700 🕐 From 8PM

CASINO TAORO
Tenerife's grandest casino
is housed in a former hotel
that played host to
Europe's nobility over a
century ago. Cocktails,
restaurant and slot
machines, as well as
roulette and gambling
tables. Smart dress only.
There's a modest entrance
charge and you must take
your passport.
✉ Parque Taoro, Puerto de la
Cruz ☎ 922 380550 🕐 From
8PM

PUBS, CLUBS & DISCOS

LOS CRISTIANOS

AQUARIUM
✉ Avenida de Suecia, Los
Cristianos

PLAYA DE LAS AMÉRICAS

Las Veronicas, on the
seafront road in Playa de
las Américas is the focal
point for entertainment. It
livens up around 11PM,
bars close 3AM–6AM.

BANANA GARDEN
A (slightly) older group
prefers this show and
restaurant venue.
✉ Veronicas, Playa de las
Américas ☎ 922 790365

BYBLOS
✉ Hotel Columbus, Playa de las
Américas

LINEKERS BAR
Bar food and TV at this
noisily popular laddish
football pub.
✉ Centro Comercial Starco,
Playa de las Américas

METROPOLIS
A popular pub-disco, with
house and live music.
✉ Hotel Conquistador, Paseo
Maritimo, Playa de las Américas
☎ 922 797359

PRISMAS
✉ Hotel Tenerife Sol, Playa de
las Américas ☎ 922 790371

TRAUMA
✉ Centro Comercial Palm Beach,
Avenida Litoral, Playa de las
Américas ☎ 922 790001

PUERTO DE LA CRUZ

A quieter, slightly older
holiday crowd frequents
Puerto's late-night venues.

BLUE NOTE
A well-known jazz spot.
✉ Calle Zamora 15

QATAR
✉ Calle Aceviño, Urbanización
La Paz

CONCORDIA CLUB
✉ Avenida de Venezuela 3

JOY
✉ Obispo Pérez Cáceres

VICTORIA
✉ Hotel Tenerife Playa, Avenida de Colón

SANTA CRUZ

Santa Cruz's nightspots mainly attract young Spanish visitors and some adventurous foreign tourists.

DAIDA
✉ Calle Carlos Hamilton, Residencial Anaga

KU
✉ Parque la Granja

NOOCTUA
✉ Avenida Anaga 37

DINNER DANCE, NIGHTCLUBS & CABARET

Many places offer floorshows and entertainment while the audience is dining or drinking. Some feature international entertainers while others offer showgirls.

BARBACOA TACORANTE
Folklore show based on Tenerife's carnival, including a barbecue-style dinner.
✉ Calle Garoé, Urbanización La Paz, Peurto de la Cruz ☎ 922 382910

PUERTO DE LA CRUZ & THE WEST

ANDROMEDA
This popular, stylish cabaret and show-restaurant was created by artist César Manrique and is located on the seafront.

It attracts world-class artistes and professional dancers and showgirls.
✉ Isla del Lago, Lago Martiánez, Puerto de la Cruz ☎ 922 383852 🕐 Dinner 8PM, floor show 10PM

BARBACOA TACORANTE
Folklore show based on Tenerife's carnival with a barbecue-style dinner.
✉ Calle Garoé, Urbanización La Paz, Peurto de la Cruz ☎ 922 382910

TENERIFE PALACE
✉ Camino del Coche, Puerto de la Cruz ☎ 922 382960

PLAYA DE LAS AMÉRICAS AND THE SOUTH

LA BALLENA
A show-restaurant on the Costa del Silencio.
✉ Ten-Bel ☎ 922 730060

PIRÁMIDES DE ARONA
Gala performances featuring cabaret, opera, ballet and flamenco.
✉ Mare Nostrum Resort, Avenida de las Américas, Playa de las Américas ☎ 922 757549

TABLAO FLAMENCO
See flamenco shows while you dine.
✉ Avenida Rafael Puig Lluvina, Playa de las Américas ☎ 922 797611

THEME DINNER

CASTILLO SAN MIGUEL
Dine in jolly mood in this mock-medieval castle – family fun with music, singing and dancing.
✉ Aldea Blanca, San Miguel ☎ 922 700276

A NIGHT ON THE TOWN

In Puerto de la Cruz, nightlife is mainly focused on Avenida de Colón and its side turnings. It's relaxed, good-humoured and civilised, with live music bars and discos. In Playa de las Américas, things are livelier, more raucous and harder-edged, with the centre of action being around the Veronicas complex. Here you'll find discos for all tastes, and fun pubs and bars where things get going after 11PM. To get away from tourists, visit Santa Cruz for cheaper discos and late-night bars – look along Avenida Anaga and Rambla del General Franco. Don't miss the city's open-air discos during high summer. However, Santa Cruz tends to be quiet at night during the week, livelier at weekends.

83

TENERIFE
practical matters

WHAT YOU NEED

	UK	Germany	USA	Netherlands	Spain
● Required					
○ Suggested					
▲ Not required					
Passport/National Identity Card	●	●	●	●	▲
Visa	▲	▲	▲	▲	▲
Onward or Return Ticket	○	○	●	○	○
Health Inoculations	▲	▲	▲	▲	▲
Health Documentation (➤ 90, Health)	●	●	●	●	▲
Travel Insurance	○	○	○	○	○
Driving Licence (national with Spanish translation or International)	●	●	●	●	●
Car Insurance Certificate	●	●	●	●	●
Car Registration Document	●	●	●	●	○

WHEN TO GO

Tenerife

■ High season
■ Low season

20°C JAN	21°C FEB	23°C MAR	24°C APR	25°C MAY	27°C JUN	28°C JUL	29°C AUG	28°C SEP	26°C OCT	23°C NOV	20°C DEC

🌧 Wet   ☁ Cloud   ☀ Sun   🌦 Sunshine/Showers

TIME DIFFERENCES

GMT 12 noon	Tenerife 12 noon	California 4AM	New York 7AM	New Zealand 12 midnight	Rest of Spain 1PM

TOURIST OFFICES

In the UK
Spanish National Tourist Office
22–23 Manchester Square
London
W1M 5AP
☎ 020 74868077

In the USA
Tourist Office of Spain
665 Fifth Avenue, 35th floor
New York
NY 10103
☎ 212/265-8822

Other TOs in Chicago, Los Angeles, Miami.

ARRIVING

Almost all flights to Tenerife arrive at Reina Sofía (or Tenerife Sur) Airport (☎ 922 759200), on the Costa del Silencio near Playa de las Américas in the south of the island.

Reina Sofía Airport To Puerto de la Cruz	Journey times	
	🚆	N/A
100 kilometres	🚌	N/A
	🚗	2 hours

Los Cristianos Ferry To La Gomera	Journey times	
	🚆	N/A
	🚌	N/A
	⛴	90 mins

MONEY

The euro (€) is the official currency of Spain. Euro banknotes and coins were introduced in January 2002. Banknotes are issued in denominations of 5, 10, 20, 50, 100, 200 and 500 euros; coins in denominations of 1, 2, 5, 10, 20 and 50 cents, and 1 and 2 euros.
Euro traveller's cheques are widely accepted, as are all major credit cards. Credit and debit cards can also be used to withdraw euro notes from ATMs. Spain's former currency, the peseta, went out of circulation in February 2002.

TIME

The time in Tenerife (and all the Canary Islands) is the same as in the UK. Sometimes a temporary 1-hour time difference occurs when clocks go forward or back in March and September. The Canary Islands are 5 hours ahead of the eastern US.

CUSTOMS

There are no restrictions at all on goods taken into Tenerife or other Canary Islands.

It would be pointless to take most goods into these islands in the expectation of saving money, however: almost everything is cheaper in the Canaries than it is at home. If you are carrying a large amount of money, you should declare it on arrival to avoid explanations on departure.

The customs allowances for travellers arriving in the UK from the Canary Islands are:
200 cigarettes; or
100 cigarillos; or
50 cigars; or
250gms of tobacco
2 litres of still table wine
1 litre of spirits or strong liqueurs over 22%volume; or
2 litres of fortified wine, sparkling wine or other liqueurs
60ml of perfume
250ml of toilet water
£145 worth of all other goods including giftsand souvenirs.

Travellers under 17 are not allowed to bring in tobacco and alcohol.

There are a few obvious exceptions to the information above, notably illegal drugs, firearms, obscene material and unlicensed animals.

EMBASSIES & CONSULATES

UK
Santa Cruz
☎ 922 286863

Germany
Santa Cruz
☎ 922 286950

USA
Santa Cruz
☎ 922 284812

Canada
Madrid
☎ 01 4314556

TOURIST OFFICES

- **Tenerife**
  Garachico
  Calle Estéban de Ponte 5
  ☎ 922 133461

  Los Cristianos
  Centro Cultural, Plaza del Carmen
  ☎ 922 757137

  Los Gigantes
  Edificio Seguro del Sol 36–37,
  Playa de la Arena
  ☎ 922 860348

  Playa de las Américas
  Centro Comercial
  City Centre
  ☎ 922 797668

  Puerto de la Cruz
  Plaza de Europa 5
  ☎ 922 386000

  Santa Cruz
  Palacio Insular (ground floor),
  Plaza de España
  ☎ 922 239592

- **La Gomera**
  Playa de Santiago
  Edificio las Vistas, Local 8,
  Avenida Marítima
  ☎ 922 895650

  San Sebastián
  Calle Real 4
  ☎ 922 141512

- **Websites**
  Spanish National Tourist Office:
  www.tourspain.es

  Local information:
  www.cabtfe.es/puntoinfo
  www.canary-isles.com
  www.ecanarias.com
  www.webtenerife.com

NATIONAL HOLIDAYS

J	F	M	A	M	J	J	A	S	O	N	D
2	1	1	(3)	1	(1)	1	1		1	1	3

1 Jan	Año Nuevo (New Year's Day)
6 Jan	Los Reyes (Epiphany)
2 Feb	La Candelaria (Candlemas)
19 Mar	San José (St Joseph's Day)
Mar/Apr	Pascua (Easter) Thu, Fri, Sun of Easter Week, and following Mon
1 May	Día del Trabajo (Labour Day)
May/Jun	Corpus Christi
25 Jul	Santiago (St James' Day)
15 Aug	Asunción (Assumption)
12 Oct	Hispanidad (Columbus Day)
1 Nov	Todos los Santos (All Saints' Day)
6 Dec	Constitución (Constitution Day)
8 Dec	Immaculada Concepción (Immaculate Conception)
25 Dec	Navidad (Christmas)

OPENING HOURS

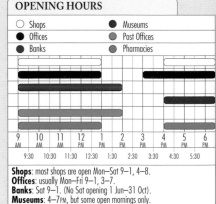

○ Shops	● Museums
● Offices	● Post Offices
● Banks	● Pharmacies

9 AM	10 AM	11 AM	12 PM	1 PM	2 PM	3 PM	4 PM	5 PM	6 PM
9:30	10:30	11:30	12:30	1:30	2:30	3:30	4:30	5:30	

Shops: most shops are open Mon–Sat 9–1, 4–8.
Offices: usually Mon–Fri 9–1, 3–7.
Banks: Sat 9–1. (No Sat opening 1 Jun–31 Oct).
Museums: 4–7PM, but some open mornings only.
Post Offices: Mon–Sat 9–2.
Pharmacies: as shops but closed Sat afternoons. Normally at least one open after hrs (rota on door).
Restaurants: lunch, noon–3PM; dinner 7PM– late.

ELECTRICITY

The voltage is 220–225v

Sockets take the standard European two-round-pin plugs. Bring an adaptor for any British or American appliances you wish to use with their usual plugs, and Americans should change the voltage setting on appliances, or bring a voltage transformer.

TIPS/GRATUITIES

Yes ✓ No ✗		
Hotels & Restaurants	✗	Inc
Room service	✓	€1–2
Café/bar	✓	change
Taxis	✓	10%
Porters	✓	€1–2
Chambermaids	✓	€1–2
Ushers/usherettes at shows & events	✓	change
Hairdressers (women's)	✓	€2–3
Cloakroom/washroom attendant	✓	50c
Tour guide	✗	€2–3

PUBLIC TRANSPORT

Domestic Flights
Los Rodeos (or Tenerife Norte) Airport (☎ 922 6359880), at La Laguna in the north of the island, is used for domestic inter-island flights. (➤ 87, Arriving). Flights to La Gomera will eventually use a new airport at Playa de Santiago in the south of the island, but at present services are restricted.

Buses
Buses are called locally *guaguas* (pronounced wah-wahs). The stops are called *paradas* and are indicated by a letter P. A bus station is called an *estación de guaguas*. Most Tenerife buses are operated by TITSA. Services are fairly frequent and inexpensive on main routes between towns. Off the main roads, and throughout La Gomera, service is intermittent and generally of little use to visitors. If you plan to use buses a lot, save up to 50 per cent by purchasing a multi-trip TITSA Bono-Bus card. TITSA hotline (English language) ☎ 922 531300

Ferries
Transmediterránea (59 Calle La Marina 59, Santa Cruz ☎ 922 277300): ferries from Santa Cruz to mainland Spain and other Canary Islands; car and passenger ferries from Los Cristianos to La Gomera.
Estación Jet-Foil (Muelle Norte, Santa Cruz ☎ 922 243012): jetfoil to Las Palmas de Gran Canaria (80 minutes).
Estación Hidro-Foil (☎ 922 796178): hydrofoils from Los Cristianos to La Gomera (35 mins).
Ferry Gomera (☎ 922 790215): car and passenger ferries from Los Cristianos to La Gomera (90 mins).
Fred Olsen (Ticket office, Muelle Ribera, Santa Cruz ☎ 922 628200): frequently from Los Christianos and Santa Cruz to La Gomera and Gran Canaria.

CAR RENTAL

It is relatively inexpensive to hire a car on Tenerife, but pricier on La Gomera. The small local car firms are efficient (ask for an after-hours emergency number), though the international firms are represented. Drivers must be over 21. A good road map is essential.

TAXIS

Cabs display a special SP licence plate (*servicio público*). Some taxi ranks display fares between principal destinations. In addition, taxi drivers offer island tours for up to four passengers; negotiate the fare before you set off.

DRIVING

Speed limit on motorways:
100–120kph

Speed limit on other main roads:
100kph

Speed limit in towns:
40kph

Seat belts are compulsory for all passengers. Children under 10 (excluding babies in rear-facing baby seats) must ride in the back seats. If you need child seats, it is strongly advised to book ahead.

Drink-driving: Driving under the influence of alcohol is strictly illegal and random breath tests are carried out; the consequences of being involved in an accident could result in a jail term.

Petrol: Unleaded petrol (*sin plomo*) is the norm. Petrol stations on main roads are usually open 24hrs and most take credit cards. Off main roads, they may be far apart, closed on Sun, and don't always take credit cards.

Hired cars and their drivers should all be insured by the hire company. In the event of a breakdown, call the car hire company's emergency number.
Fines: hefty on-the-spot fines are levied for not wearing seat belts, not stopping at a Stop sign or overtaking where forbidden.

HOSPITALS & CLINICS

Hotels can generally access medical assistance quickly in an emergency.

Santa Cruz
Hospital General de Tenerife, Santa Cruz ☎ 922 790401
Hospital Nuestra Señor de Candelaria, Santa Cruz ☎ 922 275563
Puerto de la Cruz and the North
24-hour English-speaking doctors ☎ 900 100090 (free call)
Medical Centre ☎ 900 100090 (free call)
Playa de las Américas and the South
Centros Medicos del Sur Carretera Gen. del Sur, Playa de las Américas; 24-hour English-speaking doctors ☎ 922 791000

PHOTOGRAPHY

What to Photograph: Pico del Teide is the ever-changing presence in many Tenerife views. The Teide National Park provides extraordinary images, as landscapes or close up. Lush colourful vegetation makes a startling backdrop for holiday snaps.
Film: Most popular brands of colour or transparency film are readily available — others may be harder to find. Developing is cheaper in the UK.

PERSONAL SAFETY

Street crime is quite rare in Tenerife and La Gomera but visitors should not be complacent. Uniformed police are always present in tourist areas. The greatest risk is assault or theft by another tourist. Lock doors and windows before going out. Put all valuables in the boot of your car.

- Fire is a risk in hotels – locate the nearest fire exit to your room and ensure it is not blocked or locked.
- Do not leave possessions unattended on the beach or in cars.

Police assistance:
☎ **091** from any call box

TELEPHONES

To call the operator, dial 1009. To use a phone in a bar, simply pay the charge requested at the end of the call – the barman has a meter to check the cost. To use a public pay phone, you'll usually need *una tarjeta de teléfono*, a phone card – available from tobacconists and similar shops. There are also phone offices marked Telefónica Internacional where you pay a clerk after the call.

International Dialling Codes
First dial 00, wait for a change of tone, then dial the country code:

UK	44
Ireland	353
USA	1
Spain	number only

POST

Postboxes are yellow, and often have a slot marked *Extranjeros* for mail to foreign countries. Letters and postcards to the UK: 50c (up to 20gms). Air letters and postcards to the US/Canada: 75c (up to 15gms). Letters within Spain: 20c.
Buy stamps at tobacconists, souvenir shops or post offices (*correos y telegrafos*).

HEALTH

Insurance
Nationals of EU and certain other countries can get medical treatment with the relevant documentation (Form E111 for Britons), although private medical insurance is still advised and is essential for all other visitors.

Dental Services
Emergency treatment can be expensive but is covered by most medical insurance (but not by Form E111). Hotel receptionists and holiday reps can generally advise on a local dentist.

Sun Advice
Remember that the Canaries are 700 miles nearer the Equator than southern Spain – on the same latitude as the Sahara. Use generous amounts of sun cream with a high protection factor. A wide-brimmed hat and a T-shirt (even when swimming) are advisable for children.

Drugs
Any essential prescribed medications should be taken with you to Tenerife or La Gomera. The well-known over-the-counter proprietary brands of analgesics and popular remedies are available at all pharmacies. All medicines must be paid for, even if prescribed by a doctor.

Safe Water
Tap water is safe all over the islands, except where signs indicate otherwise. The taste may be slightly salty. Bottled water is recommended.

LANGUAGE

People working in the tourist industry, including waiters, generally know some English. In places where few tourists venture, including bars and restaurants in Santa Cruz, it is helpful to know some basic Spanish.

Pronunciation guide: *b* almost like a *v*; *c* before *e* or *i* sounds like *th* otherwise like *k*; *d* can be like English *d* or like a *th*; *g* before *e* or *i* is a guttural *h*, between vowels like *h*, otherwise like *g*; *h* always silent; *j* guttural *h*; *ll* like English *lli* (as in 'million'); *ñ* sounds like *ni* in 'onion'; *qu* sound like *k*; *v* sounds a little like *b*; *z* like English *th*.

hotel	*hotel*	breakfast	*el desayuno*
room	*una habitación*	bathroom	*el cuarto de baño*
single/double/	*individual/doble/*	shower	*la ducha*
twin	*con dos camas*	balcony	*el balcón*
one person	*una persona*	key	*la llave*
one/two nights	*una noche/dos noches*	reception	*la recepción*
reservation	*una reserva*	room service	*el servicio de*
rate	*la tarifa*		*habitaciones*

bureau de change	*cambio*	pounds sterling	*libras esterlinas*
post office	*correos*	US dollars	*dólares*
cash machine/	*cajero*	banknote	*un billete de banco*
ATM	*automático*	traveller's	*cheques de*
foreign exchange	*cambio (de divisas)*	cheques	*viaje*
foreign currency	*cambio*	credit card	*la tarjeta de crédito*

restaurant	*restaurante*	cheers!	*salud!*
cafe-bar	*bar*	dessert	*el postre*
table	*una mesa*	water	*agua*
menu	*la carta*	(house) wine	*vino (de la casa)*
set main	*plato*	beer	*cerveza*
course	*combinado*	drink	*la bebida*
today's set menu	*el plato del día*	bill	*la cuenta*
wine list	*la carta de vinos*	toilets	*los servicios*

plane	*el avion*	single/return ...	*una ida/*
airport	*el aeropuerto*		*de ida y vuelta*
bus	*el guagua/*	ticket office	*el despacho de*
	autobús		*billetes*
ferry	*el ferry*	timetable	*el horario*
terminal	*terminus*	seat	*un asiento*
ticket	*un billete*	reserved seat	*un asiento reservado*

yes	*si*	Is there ...? Do you	*Hay ...?*
no	*no*	have ...?	
please	*por favor*	I don't speak	*No hablo*
thank you	*gracias*	Spanish	*español*
Hello/hi	*Hola!*	I am ...	*Soy ...*
Hello/good day	*Buenos días*	I have ...	*Tengo ...*
Sorry, pardon me	*Perdon*	Help!	*Socorro!*
Bye, see you	*Hasta luego*	How much?	*Cuánto es?*
that's fine	*está bien*	open	*abierto*
What?	*Como?*	closed	*cerrado*

REMEMBER

● Reconfirm your return flight with the airline or holiday rep at least one day before departure.

● Check in at least 90 minutes before flight departure.

● Allow time to return your care hire.

Index

TwinPack
Tenerife

Written by   Andrew Sanger
Updated by   Lindsay Hunt
Edited, designed and produced by AA Publishing
Maps   © Automobile Association Developments Limited 2002
Fold-out map   © Freytag–Berndt u. Artaria KG, 1231 Vienna–Austria, all rights reserved

Published and distributed by AA Publishing, a trading name of Automobile Association
Developments Limited, whose registered office is Millstream, Maidenhead Road, Windsor,
Berkshire SL4 5GD. Registered number 1878835.

The contents are believed correct at the time of printing. Nevertheless, the publishers cannot be
held responsible for any errors or omissions or for changes in the details given in this guide or for
the consequences of any reliance on the information it provides. Assessments of attractions,
hotels, restaurants and other sights are based upon the author's personal experience and,
therefore, necessarily contain elements of subjective opinion which may not reflect the
publishers' opinion or dictate a reader's own experiences on another occasion.

We have tried to ensure accuracy in this guide, but things do change and we would be grateful if
readers would advise us of any inaccuracies they may encounter.

A CIP catalogue record for this book is available from the British Library.

ISBN 0 7495 3460 5

Colour separation by Chroma Graphics Overseas (PTE) Limited, Singapore
Printed and bound by Times Publishing Group,

ACKNOWLEDGEMENTS
The Automobile Association wishes to thank the following photographers and libraries for their
assistance in the preparation of this book:
INTERNATIONAL PHOTOBANK f/cover (c) Bibibeca Vell; POWERSTOCK/ZEFA f/cover (b) girl at fair;
MRI BANKERS' GUIDE TO FOREIGN CURRENCY 87

All the remaining pictures used in this publication are held in the Automobile Association's own
photo library (AA Photo Library) and were taken by the following photographers:
P BENNETT f/cover bottom parasols; C JONES f/cover (d) dolphin show, 13b, 35, 43t; R MOORE
f/cover (e) festival, 6, 7, 9, 12b, 14, 16t, 17, 18b, 19t, 19b, 20b, 27, 32b, 36t, 36b, 39t, 39b, 45t,
45b, 49t, 54, 55b, 57b, 85b; C SAWYER f/cover (b) waterskier, (g) parrot, b/cover sculpture, 5t, 5b,
15, 16b, 18t, 21t, 21b, 23t, 25b, 26t, 29t, 29b, 30, 31t, 31b, 32t, 33b, 37t, 37b, 38t, 38b, 41t, 41b,
42b, 43b, 44t, 46, 47b, 48t, 48b, 51t, 51b, 55t, 56, 57t, 58t, 60t, 61b; J TIMS f/cover (c)
windsurfer, (f) cactus, 1, 12t, 13t, 20t, 23b, 24t, 24b, 25t, 26b, 28t, 28b, 33t, 34t, 34b, 41t, 41b,
42t, 44c, 44b, 47, 49b, 50t, 50b, 52, 58b, 61t, 84, 85t, 90t, 90bl, 90br.

Dear **TwinPack** Traveller

Your comments, opinions and recommendations are very important to us. So please help us to improve our travel guides by taking a few minutes to complete this simple questionnaire.

You do not need a stamp (unless posted outside the UK). If you do not want to cut this page from your guide, then photocopy it or write your answers on a plain sheet of paper.

Send to: **The Editor, AA TwinPack Travel Guides, FREEPOST SCE 4598, Basingstoke RG21 4GY.**

Your recommendations…

We always encourage readers' recommendations for restaurants, nightlife or shopping – if your recommendation is used in the next edition of the guide, we will send you a *FREE* **AA TwinPack Guide** of your choice. Please state below the establishment name, location and your reasons for recommending it.

_____

_____

_____

_____

Please send me **AA TwinPack**
Cyprus ❏ Gran Canaria ❏ Lanzarote & Fuerteventura ❏ Madeira ❏
Mallorca ❏ Malta & Gozo ❏ Menorca ❏ Tenerife ❏
(*please tick as appropriate*)

About this guide…

Which title did you buy?
AA *TwinPack* _____
Where did you buy it? _____
When? m m / y y

Why did you choose an AA *TwinPack* Guide? _____

_____

_____

_____

_____

Did this guide meet your expectations?
Exceeded ❏ Met all ❏ Met most ❏ Fell below ❏
Please give your reasons _____

_____

_____

continued on next page…

Were there any aspects of this guide that you particularly liked? _____

_____

_____

_____

Is there anything we could have done better? _____

_____

_____

_____

_____

About you…

Name (*Mr/Mrs/Ms*) _____

Address _____

_____

_____ Postcode _____

Daytime tel no _____

Which age group are you in?

Under 25 ☐   25–34 ☐   35–44 ☐   45–54 ☐   55–64 ☐   65+ ☐

How many trips do you make a year?

Less than one ☐   One ☐   Two ☐   Three or more ☐

Are you an AA member? Yes ☐   No ☐

About your trip…

When did you book? m m / y y   When did you travel? m m / y y

How long did you stay? _____

Was it for business or leisure? _____

Did you buy any other travel guides for your trip?

If yes, which ones? _____

_____

Thank you for taking the time to complete this questionnaire. Please send it to us as soon as

possible, and remember, you do not need a stamp (*unless posted outside the UK*).

Happy Holidays!